HOW TO START
AND GROW AN ATM BUSINESS

THE ULTIMATE SIDE HUSTLE

I0422247

THE AMAZING MONEY MACHINE
How to Make Money Owning and Operating ATM Machines

By Noah C. Wieder

Publisher of ATMDepot.com

Disclaimer / Legal Notices / Copyright and Trademark Notices

else who is an affiliate for the mentioned product or service (individually and collectively, the "Affiliate"). The Affiliate recommends products and services in this book based in part on a good faith belief that purchasing such products or services will help readers in general.

No Earnings Projections, Promises, or Representations for purposes of this disclaimer. Any earnings or income statements, or earnings or income examples, are only estimates of what the Author thinks you could earn. Where specific income figures are used and attributed to an individual or business, those persons or businesses have earned that amount. There is no assurance you'll do as well. If you rely upon our figures, you must accept the risk of not doing as well. Any and all claims or representations regarding income earnings in this book should not be considered average earnings. There can be no assurance that any prior successes or past results as to income earnings can be used to indicate your future success or results. Financial and income results are based on many factors. We have no way of knowing how well you will do, as we do not know your background, work ethic, or business skills or practices. Therefore, we do not guarantee or imply that you will generate any passive income, do as well, or make any money. There is no assurance you'll do as well. If you rely upon our figures, you must accept the risk of not doing as well. ATM businesses and earnings derived from it have unknown risks and are unsuitable for everyone. Making decisions based on any information presented in this book should be done only with the knowledge that you could experience a loss or make no money.

The information presented in this book is for educational and informational purposes only. Use caution and seek the advice of qualified professionals. Check with your accountant, lawyer or professional advisor before acting on this or any information. The information in this book should be carefully considered and evaluated before reaching a business decision on whether to rely on them or not. You agree that the Author is not responsible for the success or failure of your business decisions relating to any information presented herein. In no event shall the Author be liable for any direct, indirect, incidental, punitive, or consequential damages of any kind whatsoever with respect to the service, the materials, and the products contained within. This book is not intended to be a substitute for professional advice.

Materials in this book may contain information that includes or is based upon forward-looking statements within the meaning of the Securities Litigation Reform Act of 1995. Forward-looking statements give the Author's expectations for forecasts of future events. You can identify these statements because they do not relate strictly to historical or current facts. They use words such as "anticipate," "believe," "estimate," "expect," "intend," "plan," "project," and other words and terms of similar meaning in connection with a description of potential earnings or financial performance. Any and all forward-looking statements here or on any materials in this book are intended to express an opinion of earnings potential. Many factors will be important in determining your actual results. And no guarantees are made that you will achieve similar results to the Author or anyone else; in fact, no guarantees are made that you will achieve any results from the Author's ideas and techniques found in this book.

DEDICATION

I dedicate this book to my mother and father. Without their unwavering support, I wouldn't be who or where I am today. Mom, Dad, I know you're still watching over me even though you're no longer with us. Thanks for always being there in good times and bad. Thank you for your continued love and support even though I was a teenage rebel.

Mom, we lost you way too soon. We miss you dearly. You were way ahead of your time. As a health nut and yoga instructor in the 1970s, I grew up knowing that you really are what you eat, even though it took me 30+ years to listen to your advice; thanks for that.

Dad, as a successful entrepreneur, you set an example and taught me that money isn't everything, but it makes you more comfortable. You instilled a sense of humor and reminded me that gratitude is vital to enjoying life. Thanks for that, even though my lousy dad puns drive my wife and kids crazy sometimes.

You taught me that nothing comes without working for it and success isn't easy. It's attainable to anyone that works hard, is dedicated, and doesn't quit too soon! Dad, you had an incredible 97 years. You're truly missed.

I love you both,
Noah

TABLE OF CONTENTS

Thank you so much for purchasing my book!
As a thank you, I'd love to offer you a FREE GIFT.

To get your gift, simply visit ATMDepot.com/gift

PREFACE

So many people have asked me how I make money with ATMs and want to know how they could do it, too, so I got the idea to author a book about the ATM business so beginners could get all the info in one place. I've been in the ATM business so long that it's second nature, and I didn't realize that so many people between the ages of 25 and 50 were interested in learning the ATM business.

Then, after explaining it, I noticed that these same folks realized how accessible the business is once they installed their first ATM. However, they were still hesitant to get started. I constantly repeated myself during phone calls and networking events, so I began writing the original Amazing Money Machine book in 2013. I recorded many conversations, which helped me organize everything I was asked to discuss about the business all in one place. I published the first edition in 2015.

In 2016 and 2017, there were a few changes in the industry. Cryptocurrency started gaining popularity, then in 2018, our Facebook group #ATMEntreprenuers became very popular, which sparked my desire to start updating the book with answers to some new questions commonly asked in the group.

The pandemic put a lot of people's plans on hold. In April 2020, my 96 years young, very healthy, and vibrant father was diagnosed with terminal bile duct cancer. It shocked all of us. I thought my father would easily live to be 100. We lost him just ten days after his 97th birthday. I was his estate trustee, which felt like a full-time job for what seemed like a year.

In 2023 the fear of the pandemic started to wane, and people are refocusing on their dreams of entrepreneurship; it is time to finish this updated version. Here it is, updated and revised.

INTRODUCTION

Did you know that over half a million automated teller machines (ATMs) currently operate in the United States? While the number continues to grow as the convenience of withdrawing cash without going to the bank continues to attract many people, there are still plenty of opportunities, even with the advent of cryptocurrency, the craze surrounding it, and crypto ATMs.

What may come as no surprise is that financial institutions like banks and credit unions don't even own most ATMs. More than half of the ATMs in operation in the USA today are owned and operated by Independent ATM Deployers (IADs), Independent Sales Organizations (ISOs), and Subcontracted ISOs (Sub-ISOs).

You will read these terms frequently throughout this book. Remember that IADs are typically ATM businesses that work with an ISO or Sub-ISO. An ISO is a registered sales organization, and a sub-ISO is an organization contracted with the ISO. An ISO is required to register with the networks and have a sponsor bank. Becoming a registered ISO can take up to a year, plus associated fees. IAD is the term that applies to anyone getting started in the ATM business that plans to deploy, own, and operate ATM machines locally.

IADs can be anyone from a single person like you to a group of individuals or even a larger company that does not want to go through the pain, headache, and expense of becoming an ISO. IADs typically invest their money in ATMs and generate income through them, or they help merchants and retailers manage their own ATMs and share in the profits.

Since there is more paper currency in circulation today than ever before, and since people in the United States will never give up cold hard cash, the demand for ATMs is unlikely to decrease anytime soon. Although there have been reports of merchants in some states going cashless, those states recently introduced legislation that prohibits merchants from not accepting cash. So setting up your ATM business can still be very lucrative, even if it's just a side hustle.

With new tax laws lowering the threshold for 1099s when receiving money digitally via apps like Cash App, Venmo, Paypal, and the like, many people prefer not to have their spending tracked, and the use of cash has been increasing despite what you might hear in social media or in the news.

Why Should You Read This Book?

First, I want to clarify that this ATM business book isn't a guide to getting rich quickly. This book will teach you how to start an ATM business and familiarize you with all of the terms and how-to information you'll need to know to go from not knowing anything about the ATM business to understanding what it means to operate an ATM business successfully.

With a successful ATM business, you can collect fees and earn money without having to go to work all the time. This book will show you how to stop trading your time for money. It's a book about how to build wealth slowly and steadily.

There are a lot of books and articles about how to make money, books about building passive income, and get-rich-quick books that all make it sound so easy. People love get-rich-quick books, yet I've never met anyone who got wealthy quickly from one. Have you?

Books that I've read about passive income talk about how to make money online. This usually requires you to learn how to sell on eBay, sell on Amazon, become an Amazon affiliate or other affiliate marketer, create ads on Facebook, write a blog and sell ad space, build an eCommerce website, create a smartphone app, build an email list, funnel leads, write sales copy, trade cryptocurrency, etc.

Whew...

If you're not interested in sitting behind a computer day and night, this book is for you.

If you're not interested in learning how to operate an online business where you'd have to learn about computers and the Internet, this book is for you.

If you don't want to deal with hiring a bunch of virtual assistants to complete all of the necessary tasks to get good search engine rankings, then this book is for you.

This book is not about trading stocks, learning about futures, or joining an MLM (and trying to convince your friends that it's fantastic ---yeah, right). It's not about buying, selling, and trading REITs. This book is not about making money by buying, flipping, or renting real estate, and it doesn't involve some other real estate venture where people try to convince you that they have a ton of cash and you just have to find the right property. There are so many ways to make money it can make your head spin, right? Well, this book is different.

This book is about making money passively by operating an ATM business. It requires a simple machine (a vending machine of sorts, where the only inventory is $10 or $20 bills) that you can purchase one time and let pay for itself over and over again, month after month, generating passive income without having to keep up with computer technology, the Internet, changes in social media, or convincing your family and friends to buy stuff from you. Wouldn't that be nice!

And, if you don't want to buy, own, or operate your ATMs, I'll even share some secrets that teach you how you can still earn a passive income in the ATM business by being a locator or a vaulter.

You've probably used an ATM before. You might have even wondered why you pay a fee at the ATM to get your own money. You're using *your* ATM card to access *your* bank account, and it is *your* money you're getting, right? You've probably considered who gets that fee and may have even assumed it was the banks.

Well, suppose you use non-bank branded ATMs (typically those in retail stores, office buildings, bars, etc.). In that case, the owner of the ATM usually gets to keep that fee (or most of it), and that fee adds up fast.

Wouldn't you like to collect that $3.00 from every person who uses YOUR ATM?

Suppose only five people use an ATM machine daily, and the fee is $3.00. That's $15 per day in fees collected. Those five people daily help the ATM owner earn $450 monthly just from one machine. If you owned and operated that ATM, that money is all yours.

Suppose you operate an ATM at a slow location. Perhaps only two or three people use it per day. With a $3.00 fee, you still get 60 - 90 monthly transactions, earning $180 - $270 monthly.

You'd have six ATMs yearly if you installed just one ATM every other month. IADs that own and operate six to twelve ATMs on a small route in average to good locations can generate $1600 - $3500 monthly or more in pure profit. Once you finish reading this book, you'll understand how it works.

After you become familiar with the basic terminology, you'll find this is one of the easiest businesses you've ever seen. You do have to remember, though, that this is not a get-rich-quick book. It will take some knowledge and a little experience to place your ATMs.

Running an ATM business does require initial work, as does anything that makes you money. But, if you focus and take learning this business seriously, you can make a lot of money. Once you start earning a passive income at the level you want, you can either continue to grow it or simply kick back and watch your money roll in.

This book is designed to help you learn the entire ATM business. It does not guarantee your success. Successful people put what they have learned into action and keep trying until they succeed. It's your responsibility to act.

"Successful people put what they have learned into action and keep trying until they succeed."

- NOAH WIEDER

Whether you want to get out of your routine 9 to 5, set up a full-fledged ATM business, or simply supplement your income and make a few extra bucks with a side hustle, investing in ATMs is a fantastic route. You'll generate a nice passive income each month on autopilot. The capital outlay required is limited. This is one of the least expensive legitimate businesses from which you can start and make money almost immediately.

You don't need significant entrepreneurial experience or learn to sell stuff online, join an MLM, pay franchise fees, or flip houses. This business is a breeze compared to those.

An ATM business is a perfect solution for those looking to make a passive income in their spare time or as a side hustle. There is excellent potential in running an ATM business properly, and that is what this book is all about.

This book will provide all the information you need to operate your ATM business successfully and how to avoid the mistakes I made when I first started.

To keep it simple, you can just start doing business as yourself. You don't need to set up an LLC business to own or operate an ATM Machine. An LLC certainly helps your credibility, but you can operate as a sole proprietor efficiently if you only want to buy a few ATMs.

The key to success is to take imperfect action and get started. You'll never get going if you wait for everything to be perfect.

Use this book as your guide. It will teach you everything about buying an ATM and making profits. From getting started with your business to learning to operate the machine, this book provides tips and instructions on virtually everything you need to know about running a successful ATM business.

The only thing I ask in return is for you to **read this entire book all the way through to the end** (and if you like it, please leave a review). Then, you'll be able to make the most of the information provided.

"The key to success is to take imperfect action and get started. If you wait for everything to be perfect, you'll never get going."

– NOAH WIEDER

AUTHOR'S HISTORY

I graduated from SUNY Brockport in 1984. Back then, it was a small 10,000-student campus in Upstate New York. I earned a Bachelor of Science in Business with a minor in Computer Science. I had no idea what to do after college or with that degree, but I knew I didn't want to stay in New York.

In the summer of 1984, I packed everything I owned into a 1978 Chevy van I spent the summer of 1983 restoring and headed west to San Diego without a job waiting for me. I was lucky enough to have a very caring family. My sister and brother-in-law had moved to San Diego a few years earlier and let me crash at their home for what was supposed to be a couple of months (it turned into nine) until I got on my feet.

Upon reaching San Diego at just 21 years old, I had no job and little savings, so I quickly needed to figure out what to do. There were no internet or job boards in the early 80s, so I perused the local San Diego Union-Tribune classifieds section. I answered a few classified ads for sales jobs.

Since my dad was a salesman for his own company, and since I aspired to do that someday, I knew I needed a lot of experience first. I quickly landed a commission-only job selling artwork door to door. (If you had a pulse, they hired you.) After several months of selling artwork door-to-door, I decided that if I could be successful in door-to-door sales, I could sell something with higher commissions.

Returning to the paper's classifieds section, I realized that every car dealer in the area advertised for salespeople. Working in a car dealership selling cars to people interested in buying a car would be much better than cold soliciting businesses door-to-door trying to sell artwork.

I took a sales position with a local Toyota dealer selling used cars. (Yep, I was officially a used car salesman.) As a car guy, I enjoyed talking to people about their vehicles and current car problems. Without knowing it then, I was actually offering them a solution to their existing car woes. Selling cars seemed easy and enjoyable for a while. I did very well in my first year and was honored as car salesman of the month in March of 1985 for the most cars sold. (Wow, that was a while ago....)

Since I didn't envision myself being a car salesman forever, although it was good money for a guy in his 20s, it was not that fulfilling. Plus, it became very competitive against the career salesmen. I think management hired young, hungry salespeople to keep the seasoned career car salesmen from getting lazy.

Pursuing a job where I could use my business degree and potentially find a real career, I continued my job search. I eventually landed a job with The Price Company, which Costco acquired shortly after I left.

I worked at the Price Company (Price Club) for four years. I started at the bottom in the accounting department. I felt like I had something to prove, and since I was only making minimum wage in a union shop, I planned to climb my way up the ladder.

I eventually became an accounting supervisor, then a staff accountant, where I managed inventory shrink analysis for several warehouses. That eventually led me to the buying office, where I managed office supply and electronics inventory for dozens of warehouses. I did that for a couple of years.

While working at the Price Club was a great job, and I thought it could be a career, I really envisioned having my own company someday. I wouldn't have to answer to a boss, I could sleep in late when I wanted (I'm not a morning person), and I wanted to work towards financial freedom. After all, it is the American Dream.

I always wanted to have my own business, and with the help of a college friend (RIP, Arthur), we set out to do that in 1989 as one of the first Snapple Distributors outside of New York. Owning your business has benefits, but it also means you must do whatever it takes to get the job done.

Suffice it to say, I did not get to sleep in. I worked seven days a week, 18+ hours most days, then twenty hours a day, three days a week, when the trucks showed up with our inventory at 4:30 am. Barely one year later, the debt mounted, and we ran out of money. I eventually sold the distributorship at a loss and was tangled in a legal debt battle for the next seven months. Yuck!

That was my first of many failed attempts at entrepreneurship. However, I don't really see them as failures now. I see them as entrepreneurial learning experiences---which could fill several other books.

In 1993, after many failed business attempts and a few jobs in the merchant processing business, I got started in the ATM business. I was working for a check guarantee company when the partners formed a company called U.S. ATM.

U.S. ATM was the first distributor for a new type of ATM called a "scrip machine." Scrip machines were small countertop machines accepting

ATM cards but dispensing a voucher for cash. Once the scrip machine issued the voucher, the user took it to the cash register of the retail location or bartender if in a bar (where scrip machines were popular) to pay for his or her goods and get the difference back in cash.

Within a few months, U.S. ATM became one of the first distributors of Tidel ATM machines. A few months later, I flew to Texas and became a certified technician for Tidel ATMs throughout San Diego and Las Vegas.

Back then, we would go door to door in San Diego and Las Vegas selling Tidel AnyCard ATMs (aka Tidel Tube Machines). These were Tidel drop safes with an electronic PIN pad stuck to them with custom software. The merchant had to roll up bills and stick them in tubes that would drop out of the bottom like a vending machine.

In 1994, I was approached by the CEO of National Bankcard Association, Inc. (NBA) to run their Merchant Processing sales division. Upon successfully re-launching their merchant sales division, a year later I co-founded XtraCash ATM as a subsidiary of NBA.

NBA started to proliferate, which eventually led to an investment by venture capitalist firm John Moores Investments (JMI). (John served on the NBA board until it was sold in 2000.) We quickly grew from just fourteen employees to over 100 within a few years.

During the mid to late 90s, I was fortunate to be one of a select few individuals appointed to the first-ever Triton Advisory Committee. I served two years in that capacity. Triton is still a leader in ATM manufacturing today and is the only ATM in the world still proudly made in the USA.

As part of the XtraCash growth strategy, I trained hundreds of individuals, conducted dozens of sales training and coaching seminars for ATM distributors, and successfully negotiated contracts representing thousands of locations, including 170+ Southern California McDonald's locations.

XtraCash ATM became one of the top five ATM companies in the country at that time, managing close to 5,000 ATMs in just five years.

In 2000, XtraCash ATM was sold to the Canadian Imperial Bank of Commerce (CIBC), a prominent Canadian Bank. They wanted to use our network of ATMs as access points for their newly launched Internet Bank called Amicus.

In 2001 I wrote an article, "Are ATMs the New Plastic?" featured in Transaction World, which discusses the rise in ISO opportunities in the industry then.

In 2002, CIBC's plans changed, and they closed Amicus and sold off the ATM division to E*Trade. I was invited to join the E*Trade team in Arlington, Virginia; however, I preferred to stay in San Diego.

I spent the next year taking everything I learned over the previous decade and putting that experience to work to develop a new and better way to help others become independent ATM deployers (IADs).

In 2003, I launched ATMDepot.com, which currently helps over a thousand IADs successfully operate ATMs nationwide. Now, our family of IADs manages several thousand ATMs, and our ATM network dispenses tens of millions of dollars in ATM cash to their customers.

I am a serial entrepreneur, tech geek, father, husband, speaker, publisher, and author. I have been in the ATM business since 1993 and built two successful ATM businesses from the ground up.

I am currently the CEO of Intelligent eCommerce, Inc. which began as Wieder Marketing Int'l in 1994. I am also the CEO of Searchbug, Inc., a SaaS data provider for data enhancement, validation, and verification.

I reside in San Diego, California, with my wife and two sons, and can sometimes be spotted riding my bicycle to the office.

So, why am I telling you all of this? I am simply trying to relate that my experience validates the information I've presented on this book's pages.

I really enjoy teaching what I do and have taught thousands of people how to operate an ATM business. I put all my ATM teachings into a book about the business to help as many people as possible. The book was published in 2015. Several years later, it was time to update the original text due to changes in the ATM industry. This book is designed with you in mind.

This book compiles the last 30 years of my experience in the ATM business, hoping that it can help you build wealth through a healthy passive income by deploying ATMs in your city.

Building a nice residual income doesn't take thousands or even hundreds of machines. As you'll find, you can start your passive income now with as little as one machine, or you can even start making a passive income in the ATM business without owning any ATMs, but you'll have to finish the book to find out about all your options.

If you are really serious about earning an income with a great side hustle, it's time to start an ATM business. I sincerely hope you read all the way through this book and that my experience can put more money into your pocket and help you avoid costly mistakes.

Throughout this book, I mention several resources, most of which you can find on my website should you want to work with my team and me. I also include references to other ATM service providers in the resource section at the end. This book, and the tools I provide to support you, offer the best of everything I've heard, seen, studied, and experienced. Please use them to your advantage.

GETTING STARTED

Before moving on to the business side of things, it is essential to familiarize yourself with the process of running an ATM business and some of the terminology. On the surface, it seems like you have to sell ATMs to make money. However, this isn't necessarily the case. While you can do that if you want, the most lucrative and highest income opportunity is purchasing an ATM, installing it at a good location, and operating it yourself. You become the bank, ATM owner and operator, and independent ATM deployer (IAD). An IAD typically contracts with an ISO or Sub-ISO as their ATM vendor, depending on the service levels available or needed. Many direct processors will only work with ISOs that have their own sponsor bank. IADs can often get lower fees and better service from a Sub-ISO with a long partnership with an ISO.

You make money every time your ATM is used. Don't consider this a get-rich-quick scheme. This is a legitimate business opportunity where you can make a decent return on investment (ROI). It does require you to work at it, if only a few hours a week, to be successful.

Many IADs earn an annualized return of 35% - 70% or more. Banks pay relatively low-interest rates in comparison, so there isn't much opportunity for building wealth by keeping money in a bank. The stock market fluctuates, and bonds and mutual funds go up and down; real estate investing is great in numerous ways, but it can also be risky, and there's a big learning curve. Why invest in someone else's dream when you can invest in yourself?

More and more smart investors are turning to owning their own ATM machines. It's pretty simple, really. The beautiful thing about this business is how fast you start making money without having to invest too much money in the first place. There is one caveat: the longer you wait to begin your ATM business, the longer it takes to build your passive income, and the more competition you could face in your area.

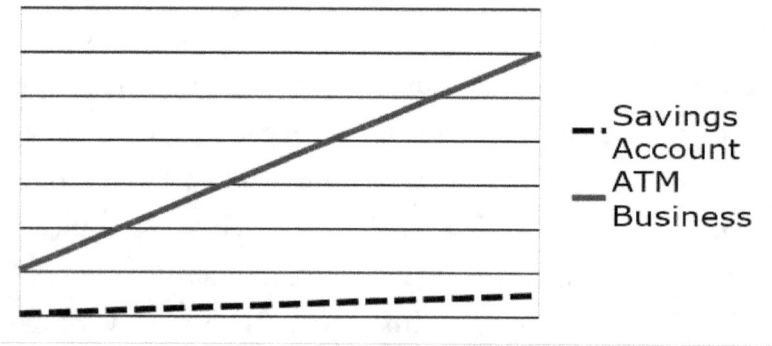

So let's look at some of the basics of how an ATM business works.

How the ATM Business Works

There is a surprising lack of awareness about the ATM business. The general perception is that banks and other financial institutions operate ATMs, so most people don't even bother inquiring about them. Most ATM businesses are actually run independently. Though more IADs are stepping into the arena, there are still no major barriers to entry, and it's a low-cost business to start.

The time is ripe for you to consider having your own ATM business. However, before that, you need to know how the business works. There are five steps involved in setting up an ATM business:

Step 1: Completing your IAD Paperwork & Setting Up a Bank Account

Every business has some type of documentation that needs to be filled out. While you don't need a specific license to operate an ATM business, you must still complete an agreement with an ATM processor or ATM vendor (ISO or Sub-ISO).

The most common way new IADs start is to create a sole proprietorship or an LLC and get a fictitious business name, a "doing business as" (DBA), so that you can open a bank account for your business. This should not be a complicated process, depending on your provider. It sets up your vendor relationship for your business.

The IAD agreement, or a standard ATM processing agreement, defines each party's responsibility for the ordinary course of business. Before you complete your IAD agreement, you'll want to pick a name for your business if you don't have one already. Some ATM processors may be willing to list you on their website in a directory in the city where you're located, but most don't. The ones that do typically charge an annual fee since it gives your local company instant credibility. This is especially useful when you're brand new and want to use the ISO, Sub-ISO, or processor clout to get leads in your area. The fees associated with being listed on an established website are sometimes worth it (as long as the website has good domain authority with real-proven traffic) because you gain instant trust. You can optimize the URL you are listed on in social media and local ads without building your own website. If you pursue this, read the rights and usage agreement carefully. You don't want to breach it and lose the URL listing. Do not buy into an ATM franchise where you can run into hidden requirements and ongoing fees.

Step 2: Choosing a Location

As every successful business does, you must spot a market gap. Every successful entrepreneur can see the potential. You should be able to find locations near where you live, work, or play that can use an ATM.

It could be a nail salon, barber shop, tattoo shop, retail store, restaurant, nightclub, adult store, shopping arcade, commercial building, manufacturing facility, festival, event, or any other place people go. The best businesses are cash-only locations or those that have a high rate of cash-paying customers. The key is determining whether there is enough foot traffic to make it profitable.

Other opportunities are locations around you that already have ATMs but where the equipment may be old, outdated, non-compliant, out of order often, or owned and operated by someone who is no longer maintaining it. People sometimes go through life-changing circumstances such as divorce, health, or family issues.

Therefore, the "gap" becomes the location where you think an ATM is needed, the location wants a newer ATM, the ownership has changed, or whoever is in charge wants to work with a different person for whatever reason.

Step 3: Buying an ATM

The next step is buying an ATM. There are many ATM companies that sell these machines, so it shouldn't be too difficult for you to find and select one. A simple online search is all it takes to contact an ATM company, but how do you know which one? I added my contact information in the resource section at the end of this book and other trusted ATM providers for reference. You can place an order for the machine, which will then be delivered to you at a specified place at an agreed-upon date and time. Once you have an ATM, the fun begins.

Step 4: Programming & Installing the Machine

The ATM has to be programmed (or re-programmed if you buy a used model or take over the management of a previously installed one) for processing. Without ATM processing, people won't be able to withdraw money from the ATM---rendering it worthless. If you're far from tech-savvy, you can request the manufacturer program the ATM before it ships, or you can coordinate with your vendor to hire a professional to program the machine on-site so you can learn. If you contact an ATM company offering ATM processing, you will complete the required paperwork to set up your machine in their system. Then you or a technician will obtain programming instructions. That is when you will get your machine's unique Terminal ID Number (TID). The ATM company's installer can do the installation, or you can decide to unbox the ATM and bolt it to the floor yourself.

Step 5: Loading the Cash

The last step is loading the machine with cash. You need to have sufficient funds— cash—in the ATM for people to withdraw the amount they need. Up until 2012, the average withdrawal transaction was $60; now, it's a little closer to $80 and can be higher if the surcharge is high. People want to maximize the withdrawal amount if they get charged a lot. If your average withdrawal is over $200, I recommend setting the surcharge as a flat rate or a percentage, whichever is greater. It will make you more money. More on that later.

Regardless, you'll need to know the capacity of the ATM you have purchased in terms of the amount of money it can hold. Most deployers buy ATMs that come standard with a 700- or 1,700-note cassette. Unless your ATM is at a bustling location, you would rarely need to fill the ATM to capacity. We'll discuss cash needs more in-depth later, but the reality is that you can start with as little as 100 or so $20 bills and then use your online portal reports and text alerts to tell you when you need to add more cash.

These five steps illustrate how the ATM business works. You buy the machine and set it up at a location of your choice. The ATM is then made available to the public, and they can use it to withdraw cash from their checking, savings, or other accounts associated with the ATM card used. You will receive a surcharge fee, which you choose and set, for each cash withdrawal transaction made on your ATM. This is your revenue from the business. It is only a matter of time before your revenue increases to the point that your original investment is recouped and you start making a big profit.

Remember that this is a basic premise of how the ATM business works. There is more to this than simply buying and installing a machine. You must complete the required banking paperwork, provide proper documentation, and pass a basic background check. As long as you have not committed a felony or financial crime, you will likely pass. If you've been convicted of a financial-related crime, find a partner or have your spouse apply to start the business. While the ATM business is pretty simple, some issues may arise from time to time, as with any business.

But don't let that discourage you. Running an ATM business may sound complex, but in reality, it's quite easy. Only a little business-like activity is involved, and you don't have to make many tough decisions; it's mostly meeting store owners, asking them to let you place an ATM in their store to help them lower credit card fees and give customers access to cash to spend more. However, if you have doubts, reading this book until the end will surely quell them. All of the information you need about operating an ATM business is provided here. So you shouldn't run into any unknown issues or face too many hassles once your business is up and running.

How You Make Money in the ATM Business

Now that you know a little bit about how the ATM business works, it is time to discuss how you make money. Keep in mind that while the business is highly lucrative, and you can build wealth, you need to keep it professional. Do things the right way, and don't create shortcuts. Don't treat your business like a hobby. It's a real business. Wherever you place your ATMs, those business people will count on you. **It's your reputation and networking skills that will help to grow your business.** Technically, there are two ways in which you can make money from an ATM:

1. ATM Surcharge

If you choose, and most ATM owners do, you will levy a fee on the transactions people perform on the ATM you own; this is called the surcharge. For instance, if someone withdraws $100 from his or her checking or savings account using your ATM, a fee would be charged, usually $2.50 - $3.50. Now you can even add a percent of the amount withdrawn. We suggest you adhere to what other ATMs in the area are charging, but I'll talk about this more later. You earn this surcharge since you are providing a service because you are saving people a trip to their bank to get cash. There are some ways you can increase the surcharge and usage, which I'll discuss later.

2. ATM Interchange

ATM networks impose interchange on banks to interconnect their bank with other ATMs. ISOs typically receive a portion of the interchange. That's how you can get 100% of the surcharge. They run their business on the interchange.

Suppose you're a Sub-ISO or IAD processing a very high volume of transactions (usually tens to hundreds of thousands) and do not need much support or accounting. In that case, you might be able to get a share of the fee charged by the network your ATM is connected to (the interchange). In this case, you may receive a few additional cents on cash withdrawal transactions from the ATM company processing your transactions. This also depends on the ATM network, which is determined based on the cardholder's ATM card, thus increasing your earnings over time.

Some ATM companies don't even mention the word interchange to their clients, while some ATM companies believe in transparency and work more like a partnership. Your success is their success. If the ATM ISO or Sub-ISO you work with shares some interchange, they will also probably pass on any fees, including onboarding, transaction, statement, or monthly minimums. So, if you receive any interchange, expect fees to be associated. Your ISO or sub-ISO must charge you something if you get the surcharge and some or all the interchange to stay in business.

In most cases, the fees are often less than the share of interchange, but this also depends on the type of ATM cards used at your location. You can always discuss the best strategy with your ATM processor once your ATMs have a track record and some transaction history. As a new IAD or an ATM beginner, it's much easier to learn and calculate income if you don't worry about fees and just get 100% of the surcharge when the ATM is used.

A true partner will want you to be able to maximize your revenue while at the same time making money for everyone involved. Remember that you want to ensure your ATM provider is making money so that they answer the phones and reply to emails when you need help. This is where an experienced ATM processor or service provider is critical. Working with a more significant ISO or Sub-ISO lets you utilize their economies of scale.

These two ways of making money through an ATM business aren't mutually exclusive. They exist simultaneously, enabling you to earn more than the basic surcharge or helping to offset some of the network fees imposed on ATM transactions. Some networks, particularly the national networks, Plus and Cirrus, have a tiered interchange structure and charge issuing banks an acquirer fee. So, depending on the actual type of card used, the interchange and acquirer fees vary. International transactions cannot be surcharged and impose a completely different set of fees. (This rarely affects regular ATMs unless you have one in a tourist-driven area.) Some ATM processing companies pass all network-related costs through to the ATM owner or whoever collects the lion's share of the surcharge.

These fees are typically minimal compared to the surcharge collected. We've seen fees range from $0.01 to $0.18 and vary by network or ATM card used. Since ATM owners don't typically bear any backend communication costs, bank sponsorship costs, or any other operational costs to complete ATM transactions, the fees generated from the ATM are pure profit which, even after some minimal processing fees, deliver a great ROI. You should not be charged any processing fees if you're getting 100% of the surcharge and no interchange.

So, how much money can you expect to make in a month through your ATM business? Well, the typical surcharge depends on your area and what you decide. However, I typically earn between $2.50 and $3.50 and, as stated earlier, a percentage on a few as well on each of my ATMs. To calculate your gross monthly revenue, you simply multiply your surcharge amount by the number of transactions you expect to perform on your ATM.

A very reasonable figure to use when estimating the number of surcharge transactions performed on an average non-bank ATM is 120 - 150 per month. This means that just four or five people have to perform a surcharge cash withdrawal transaction, on average, every day. That being said, several factors determine the number of transactions performed. For instance, if your ATM is located in a place where the foot traffic is heavy and people spend a lot of cash, you may get over twenty transactions performed daily.

So, in this example, we'll say 150 transactions are performed on your ATM in a given month, and your surcharge is $3.00; your monthly gross revenue from just one ATM would be approximately $450. While I know many online ATM Coaches try to tell you the average is 10 uses per day or 300 per month, that is on the high side. We do have ATMs performing at that level, and we even have a few doing thousands of monthly transactions. Heck, we've got an airport that does 250 per day and a seasonal ice cream shop in a heavy tourist area that does 150 per day for most of the summer and some of the fall, but then it drops to nothing in the winter since they close. So, averages are based on your experience. I prefer to under-promise and over-deliver, not the other way around.

This is a great way to earn a passive income without doing much. Your ATM company should provide you with the support you need to keep your ATM up and running. However, if you are seriously considering building wealth with your ATM business, you will have to increase your number of machines.

You'll need more than one machine to rely on for revenue. The more machines you have, the more money you will make. Also, it is important that you choose the location wisely. Of course, having more machines means more work, but the higher earnings and profits will justify the effort you have to put in.

There is good money to be made in an ATM business. You just need to know how to run it. Start with one machine to generate extra income to supplement the wages from your day job or, when you're ready, you can tackle more locations and make this a full-time income. Once you've learned the business, are comfortable with the operation, and have placed three or four ATM machines in your local area, we suggest you set up an LLC business if you have not done so already. Getting your business to the next level and operating a dozen ATM machines or more will likely mean your passive income will become dramatically more than your day job or most retirement investments, so you want a proper business to take advantage of all the tax breaks and protection an LLC offers.

Managing a small network of a dozen or so ATM machines is very easy. Once the ATMs are in place, all that's left to do is to count the money, load the machines, and get paid. If you're satisfied with the number of

ATMs you manage, you can kick back or decide to keep growing or sell the route if you want to cash out.

For example, if you have twelve machines averaging 150 transactions per month charging a $3.00 surcharge, you **will make over $5,000 monthly, and you could work less than 4 - 6 hours a week**. You will make money while sleeping regardless of how many ATMs you want to operate.

Pro Tip: Locations with higher withdrawal amounts can be leveraged to increase surcharge income. By adding a surcharge percentage, you can earn more revenue per transaction. Here's how:

Ask your processor (typically on the processing setup or change form) to set the surcharge amount to $3.00 or 1.5% (or 2% depending on the location), whichever is greater. If your ATM provider does not offer this option, see the resource section for my company info, and we will help you.

Once you set up your surcharge percentage, set up the ATM fast cash amounts. You can set up three preset buttons on each side of the screen for cash withdrawals. Consider the average withdrawal and your denomination when setting the ATM fast cash amounts. You want the left-side increment buttons to dispense a lower amount for the flat fee, and suggesting the lower amounts means the cash will last longer if users simply click a preset amount of $40, $60, or $80. Now, on the right-side buttons, we'll use increments that get you that percent income by using $300, $400, and $500.

When you charge $3.00 or 1.5%, users who withdraw $200 or less still generate surcharge revenue of $3.00. However, when users select to withdraw $300, $400, or $500, you'll earn 1.5% ($4.50, $6, or $7.50, respectively). If it's a tourist or destination location where there won't be many repeat customers, you can even charge $3.50 or 2%, whichever is greater. Then a $500 withdrawal would be a $10 charge. But be careful to consider your customer base and the merchant. You don't want anyone complaining about high fees. Percent surcharge can work in unmanned and higher-end locations and tourist, seasonal, and some event locations. We've seen percent surcharges in adult nightclubs, airport lounges, parking lots, car washes, and other places where people might be pressed for time and in a hurry as well as in certain other entertainment establishments. You can always consult your ATM provider to see if your location would support a surcharge percentage.

We manage several machines in high withdrawal venues (bars, parking lots, adult entertainment locations, and other affluent areas) where users want to withdraw the most they can. Since only some non-bank ATMs offer $300, $400, or even $500 withdrawal options, some users who want to maximize the amount they get when paying a fee will do so. When your users withdraw that much cash, you earn much more for offering that convenience. Remember that you must load a lot more cash into machines that provide this, but the upside is worth it.

If you plan to have your first ATM professionally installed, you can ask the installer to set that up for you. Just make sure the installer knows you will be charging a percentage option.

PAPERWORK & DOCUMENTATION

Once you have decided to set up an ATM business, it's time to order a machine. Before you can do that, there are a few things you need to figure out. First, you need to have a clear idea of the number of ATM machines you want to set up. Most ATM beginners start with one machine to get their feet wet.

Speak with your ATM provider to get the latest info on the best machines for your proposed location or to see if there are any specials, sales, or incentives for purchasing one ATM over another.

Next, you'll have to complete the necessary paperwork for purchasing the ATM and the documents for ATM processing, or you won't be able to operate it. You don't want an ATM machine delivered without the documentation to program or operate it. This is especially true if you purchase an ATM from a company that does not also provide processing or if you purchase a used ATM machine from a classified ad or online auction site like eBay or local classified sites like Craigslist. Be careful when buying a used machine. Many of them are out of compliance, and what appears to be a good deal really just leaves you with an expensive boat anchor....

The paperwork can be a potential stumbling block for someone new to the ATM business. In fact, some people even get discouraged to the extent that they reconsider their decision to start an ATM business.

However, the process itself is relatively easy. You only need to keep a few things in mind and shouldn't face any problems.

A big obstacle is unfamiliarity. However, if you know about the paperwork and documentation required ahead of time, you won't be as surprised and overwhelmed as some people get. With that in mind, here is a general overview of the paperwork required for ordering and setting up an ATM.

Paperwork for Ordering an ATM

You need to complete and sign a series of forms and contracts before you can order the machine and have it up and running. There are various reasons why completing the necessary paperwork is essential:

First, you need to prove your credentials and identity. You need to provide the relevant documentation and your ID to set up an ATM business or any business. This way, the underwriters can verify your identity and perform the required background checks. (The process is similar to getting a bank account.)

Second, you need to prove that you are legally allowed to run an ATM business. As per the banking network, if you have been convicted of a crime that was a felony in connection with any type of financial crime (bank fraud, money laundering, check fraud, or any related financial crime), you would not be allowed to operate such a business. Suppose you know you have a financial crime in your history. In that case, it's best to have a family member complete the paperwork and put the company in their name. You can have a side agreement with them, but as far as the banks are concerned, you couldn't be an owner or member of the LLC.

Completing the necessary paperwork ensures that the ATM company's sponsoring bank and processing center exercise due diligence to comply with all network regulations. You can ask your ATM provider if you have questions. Without proper business contracts, you risk losing everything you worked for. Don't let anyone in the business tell you that agreements and contracts are unnecessary. That is a big red flag.

Third, certain parts of the paperwork processing include government requirements to own and operate an ATM machine for compliance purposes. Try as you may, you cannot get around the requirements imposed by the federal government. If you don't complete and submit the necessary paperwork, you won't be able to get your business operational. Unscrupulous ATM companies may tell you otherwise for nefarious reasons. Consider why they wouldn't want to protect your interests by ensuring you know their responsibilities and have everything in writing.

I advise you to contact your ATM provider about the required forms to complete and submit before you need to order a machine. They will guide you in the right direction, virtually guaranteeing you can set up your business properly. Rather than trying on your own to get the paperwork done, you should seek professional help. Asking for help from your selected ATM vendor will ensure you complete the process quickly.

Before you submit your operator paperwork for a specific location, it is crucial that you decide on the service fee you are going to charge your customers and the currency denominations you are going to load into your machines. You will have a few options, so use the information in the following chapters to help you make an informed decision when ordering your machine.

Paperwork for Setting up an ATM

Part of the paperwork includes the Equipment Order Form. Once you have completed this form and ordered the ATM, you have to prepare to get it set up. You don't have to do much in the way of the actual installation process. The company you order the machine from will deliver, install, and program the machine as per your instructions. Some ATM providers will help train you to program the ATM yourself, saving you some of the programming fee. What you do have to do is complete and submit the relevant paperwork for setting up the machine.

You must consider a few things:

1. What will the surcharge fee be (I typically start with $3.00)?

2. What denominations do you want the ATM to dispense (usually $20s)?

3. What bank and bank account are you going to link the ATM to?

    Without having a bank you can work with, you cannot run an ATM business. You should figure this out beforehand because some banks can take from a few days to a few weeks to set up an account for the ATM business. You will need a voided check or a bank letter. I have found that speaking to your bank about your new ATM business before you start is best. Some banks have strict policies about working with companies that require a lot of cash. Be sure you are forthcoming with your bank to avoid any speed bumps on the road to success. You can read this blog that explains the best banks for the ATM business. (See the resource section for the link if you're not reading the electronic version.)

4. Will you install the ATM yourself or have a professional do it?

As far as setting up the ATM is concerned, you need to ensure that the location you select is ready and that you have obtained the proper site location placement agreement (SLA) with the location owner prior to the time the machine is delivered.

I recommend completing the required processing paperwork at the same time you order the machine, if possible. However, it's okay to have the machine delivered first if you want to get familiar with it yourself and get trained on how to program it. If the location where you are placing the ATM is nearby, you can have the ATM delivered to your home instead of the location, but be sure you have a vehicle big enough so that you can deliver it when it comes time to install it.

Contracts

Of course, where there are documents to complete, there are going to be a few contracts. First and foremost, you must complete a purchase agreement with the company you will buy the machine from unless you want to blindly place an order online without speaking with anyone. I recommend speaking to someone with the ATM vendor you select for your first order. Your ATM provider is your sole source of support and guidance; therefore, you cannot be successful without speaking and working with one. Call around and find someone you are comfortable working with.

As mentioned earlier, you will need to work with a local bank (one that you already do business with is a good start). Make an appointment with the branch manager and let him or her know you'll be starting an ATM business. The manager can walk you through opening the accounts. I used to recommend opening one checking account for each machine, but most banks don't want multiple accounts that have a balance being drawn down every week. It's a lot of work if they get audited, and they lose money on accounts with low average balances. I used to have one account for each ATM, so it was easier for accounting. That way you can track each day's deposits and balance back to your ATM journal and online reports. However, many banks now charge monthly fees for accounts with low balances, so having separate accounts may not make financial sense. Banking fees have changed dramatically over the last few years, so now I recommend using one account for all your machines. Then, you simply download the deposits from your bank automatically into QuickBooks so balancing is easier.

To balance the funds you load in the ATM, you count what is still in the ATM before you reload, run a trial cassette close to ensure they match (more on this later), add the number of bills you are adding, take that amount and add in what is still in the bank plus what is unsettled (en route back to your bank).

Lastly, you need to decide whether you're going to be loading the ATM, you're going to hire someone to do it for you, or the location manager or location owner will load the ATM. This means that each function and operation related to your ATM business requires you to have some sort of agreement outlining responsibilities.

You should require an additional contract if you contract with a third-party provider to load the ATM. No other agreement is required if you intend to perform that function yourself, which most new ATM business people do.

These are some of the contracts, documents, and forms you must complete to order and set up your ATMs. Remember these so you can breeze through them and start running your business as soon as possible.

The paperwork should not deter you. There are not that many agreements when you work with certain companies. Here's a quick summary of the required documentation:

1. The ATM Application includes location information, personal information, and information required for a background check. It is not a contract but is a required document.

2. The IAD Operator Agreement is the primary document outlining the responsibilities of the IAD and your vendor and protects both parties.

3. An Equipment Order Form is only necessary when not ordering ATMs online.

4. An ATM Processing Agreement lists each party's obligations, responsibilities, terms, and conditions; this is a required legal document.

5. An Automated Clearing House (ACH) document authorizes the processor to make deposits to your bank account for the daily settlement of funds (vault cash) and your monthly commissions. It also authorizes them to debit your account for any adjustments, discrepancies, or errors (albeit rare).

6. You'll also need a voided business check for the ACH. If your account is new or you don't have checks, you can request a bank letter on letterhead from your banker stating you have an account in good standing. You can also request a few free starter checks with your business and address preprinted.

7. Lastly, you will need a clear, legible copy of your driver's license.

Optional but recommended:

1. When you place the ATM in a third-party location, you should protect yourself with a placement agreement or Site Location Agreement (SLA). Some ATM processing companies (ISOs and Sub-ISOs) will provide you with the SLA they use as an example or template. You should be able to mark it up and use it as your own. Remember that any organization with a legitimate SLA most likely paid an attorney for it. So if you work with them, they should provide one. If you connect with a processing company that doesn't offer one, think twice about the kind of service you'll get from them. Make sure you customize all agreements with your logo. There are plenty of free online PDF editors to use.

2. If you wish, you can purchase separate ATM insurance for the machines. It's an additional expense and only protects so much. We used to insure them, but having so many locations gets expensive. I've had so few stolen in the last 20 years that self-insuring (putting money equal to the insurance payment in a savings account) is often cheaper. I make sure the locations have alarms, cameras, and decent security. An alarm in the ATM is also possible with a switch on the plastic door, which has to be breached first. See the resources section for insurance vendor suggestions.

LOCATION

Where to Find Locations

Location is perhaps the most important of all factors when running an ATM business, and selecting the right location to install a machine more or less guarantees success. Yet, many people select the wrong locations.

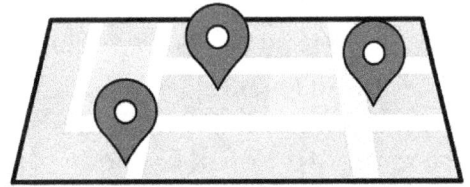

By selecting a poor location for your ATM, you end up making less money than you could, and your ROI takes longer. (That's not necessarily a bad thing unless you need more cash flow to fund growth.) However, even a poor location (I consider two transactions daily or less to be poor) can still make an annualized return of 25% - 30%. Suppose you're just looking for a good annualized return, like a CAP rate on an investment. In that case, even low transaction locations are fine.

It's hard to lose money in the ATM business, but it can still happen if you choose really poor-performing locations. The nice thing is that you can always move the ATM to a new or better place. The ATM business can be very lucrative, but only if you do the right things. Finding, selecting, and obtaining good locations should be at the top of your agenda.

Various factors determine whether or not a site is perfect for installing an ATM or not. Let's look at them:

Proximity to Nearest ATM

The first thing you have to keep in mind is the proximity of your machine to the nearest ATM location. Where can you expect a large number of people to come and use your machine? Of course, at a location where there isn't another ATM nearby.

Commercial avenues usually have several ATMs on the same street. Therefore, installing a machine there only makes sense if one or more of these factors exist: (1) you offer a lower surcharge, (2) foot traffic is high (3) nearby ATMs are old or outdated.

Proximity to Retail Outlets

People need cash when they go shopping. It is convenient for them to withdraw money while shopping and running daily errands. If your ATM can help people to save time and is more convenient than an ATM somewhere else, your ATM will be preferred. This is why setting up an ATM close to retail outlets, busy coffee shops, bars, quick service or casual restaurants, and many other establishments is a good idea. Many of these locations have ATMs already, but there are always opportunities. Many ATMs in these places may be old or outdated models needing an upgrade or the service providers have disappeared. Look for out-of-order ATMs or machines that appear to require some TLC. If you see an opportunity, inquire with the manager or store personnel to find out if there is a problem that you can help solve. The newest, best machine is good for business.

Proximity to Your Residence/Workplace

If your ATM business model requires you to load the cash into your ATMs or the locations you secure want you to be full service and load the money, it can sometimes be difficult if you live too far from your ATMs. Consider the traffic, mileage, and other costs when choosing locations. Though this might limit your business to some extent, it is best to find a location close to your home or office to start. Once you fully understand the ATM business, you can spread out. Still, there are plenty of opportunities closer than most people think. Start with a very nearby location. You can easily check the ATM occasionally until your comfort level increases. This is one way to ensure your ATM business gets off the ground and running smoothly.

Apart from these three location considerations, you also need to keep in mind the rent you may have to pay if you don't own the space where the machine will be installed. In the next section, I will provide you with a list of the best locations for installing an ATM.

Some of the Best ATM Locations

It is hard to come up with reliable estimates for the number of transactions performed at a particular ATM location. It varies by region, season, popularity, etc. For instance, an ATM in a casino usually gets more transactions on average than ATMs in other locations. Yet, some ATMs can be installed in casinos that don't get that many transactions.

Based on my experience managing thousands of ATMs, the average number of transactions one can expect from an ATM is 150 to 180 a month. That is roughly five to six transactions per day. However, plenty of locations have reported much lower and much higher monthly transactions than this—that's how you get an average. Here are some of the best ATM locations where you should consider installing a machine if you can obtain these types of venues. These venues often already have ATM machines, so it may take knowing someone or very good sales and personal skills to replace the current vendor.

Large casinos – 1,500 to 3,000 transactions (sometimes more) monthly

> Large casinos are difficult to obtain and are often controlled by banks. Still, it is not unusual to get these types of accounts depending on who you know or what you can offer. If you already work with these types of accounts offering other services, adding the ATM to your arsenal of products is a much easier way to get in the door.

Dispensaries - average 1000+ transactions monthly - Cannabis dispensaries are currently one of the fastest growing (unintended pun) locations. Since it's still federally illegal and probably will be for a few more years, it's up to each state, and retail licensing is typically announced in local cities when applications are being considered. If you can get into a dispensary, it will do well, but you will go through a lot of cash, so a percent surcharge works well here.

Smaller casinos and even some bingo halls – 300 to 800 transactions monthly Gentlemen's Clubs – 300 to 800 transactions monthly.

While gentlemen's clubs are very profitable ATM locations, they are also coveted locations and, hence, have higher competition. If you know someone at these locations or already have a relationship with these locations, it's easier to get in. Without an "in," I don't recommend starting your ATM business by approaching the locations mentioned above. Wet your feet with more easily obtainable locations and gain experience in the business, then go after more challenging locations.

The surcharge is usually higher at the three locations as mentioned earlier, making them highly lucrative and a great ROI. However, the following locations are more typical and often more easily obtainable.

Nightclubs, Bars, and Grills – 250 to 500 transactions

Barbers and Nail/Hair Salons and Tattoo Shops - 75 - 300 transactions

Believe it or not, many of these locations do quite well, and some small ones still generate enough users to have a decent ROI.

Some big locations with a lot of chairs might average eight transactions daily, resulting in 240 monthly transactions, but the average for a small place with only 4 - 6 people working will be much lower unless they are cash only.

These are locations where stylists, barbers, nail techs, and tattoo artists sometimes rent space or where there are several dozen manicurists, and the management doesn't accept credit cards due to the high fees. Also, customers like to tip in cash and often pay with cash if an ATM is nearby. If the surcharge is reasonable ($2.00), you can do quite well with larger nail salons or a salon building with many independent salon owners under one roof.

The smaller locations, with only a few stylists or artists that have fewer than 30 people per day, will be slow locations but should still produce about 50 transactions, and you can surcharge more and offer local businesses advertising to increase the revenue.

- Convenience Stores and Gas Stations – 200 to 400 transactions
- Hotels (the number of transactions depends on occupancy)
- Small – 100 to 150 transactions monthly (hotel or motel with less than 150 rooms and at least 80% occupancy)

- Medium – 100 to 200 transactions (non-branded hotels)
- Large well-known brands – over 200 transactions
- Restaurants
- Fast Food – 75 to 150 transactions
- Quick Service – 100 to 150 transactions
- Diners, Cafes, and Luncheonettes – 150 to 200 transactions

Microbreweries with Food Trucks and Parking Lots - vary depending on size but overall, typically pretty decent spots New locations are popping up everywhere you look. Think of the places you visit often or the new places opening soon that you see locally. If they seem to have a lot of patrons but don't have an ATM, that's an opportunity for you. If you go there often, so do other folks.

All transaction numbers indicated above are based on a calendar month. Based on my experience, installing an ATM at these locations yields, on average, the number of transactions mentioned, but your experience may vary. There are no guarantees that any location mentioned will meet the numbers provided. These are based solely on my experience over the last several decades I've been in the ATM business.

As you can see, the top locations are where people are more likely to spend large amounts of cash. The only issue is that most of these locations already have an ATM. Therefore, you might not find many empty spaces. Don't get discouraged. Many locations prefer a new machine over the old one they have. Plus, you can customize your ATM with special graphic packages to match the surroundings, which will surely attract customers.

While these are the best locations for profitability and revenue, you can still make a decent annual return from any location offering you 80 - 100 monthly transactions. You can enjoy a 40% to 70% annual ROI even with those monthly transaction numbers. So keep these locations in mind when trying to find spots to install your ATMs.

Check local trends and entertainment publications in print and online and subscribe to new business lists from your local or county service to locate good opportunities.

If you plan to cold call, cold walk in, or need telemarketing scripts, I'll provide a few at the end of the book. I'll also reveal how to access my private collection of other ATM sales scripts and helpful videos in the resource section so you can start negotiating location agreements. Generally, these scripts are for cold calling; however, I only recommend cold-calling store owners with "the opportunity to qualify for a free ATM placement." I don't recommend trying to close the deal over the phone; it rarely works, and you'd be wasting time. The scripts I share help you find out who the owners are so that you can call or email them to get an appointment to visit them in person to check out the business. After all, you're investing in a machine to help them increase their business. You are not selling them anything.

Adding an ATM to Your Own Retail Store

If you own a retail store, adding an ATM machine is easy and could end up being the most profitable floor space in the store. ATMs have small footprints taking up just over one square foot. Or you can install a through-the-wall machine to face the outside. This will help attract even more customers, which can increase the revenues of your business considerably. An ATM business can be highly lucrative and can bolster the revenue of your existing retail store.

Since the ATM machine will be a new addition to your business, it is essential that it is visible and well-advertised with signage so that people use it, even if they aren't planning to go into your store.

Suppose you want to draw a lot of attention to it. In that case, you can offer incentives for customers to use your machine and entice withdrawals. For instance, one of the fastest ways to build your ATM usage is to start with a very low surcharge and advertise it. Suppose you charge less than most of the competition in the area. In that case, this will definitely get people to consider using your ATM.

If you start with a low surcharge, you'll need to consider how long you will offer it. Increasing or changing your surcharge amount does not usually require the ATM to be fully reprogrammed, but sometimes new master keys will be required depending on your processor. Most ATM owners can do this themselves; however, some prefer to have a technician complete the task, so there may be a fee associated with a technician visit. Check with your ATM company before determining your surcharge amount and ask if there are any charges to change it.

There are many other ways to incentivize customers to use your ATM. Incentives can include coupons printed on the receipt or separately, depending on your equipment type. Talk to your ATM vendor about ideas and options to help you to determine the best way to monetize your ATM fully.

Since most of the newer model ATMs have large graphic screens, it is vital to work with a company that will help you take advantage of the screen of the ATM. Be sure the ATM company you work with offers custom screen graphics so you can upload your logo or other images onto your ATM to display eye-catching graphics.

Optimizing the ATM display will capture the attention of the people heading into your store so that they make a withdrawal then and there. While it is incredibly convenient for them to be able to withdraw cash from the machine when walking into the store, it is also best for you as a store owner when customers pay with cash instead of using their credit cards.

So, if you own a retail store, investing in an ATM can give your business a big boost. It not only offers convenience to your customers, but it can also lower your credit card fees by offering your customers cash, earning you big profits from surcharge fees, saving you the cost of the offset credit card charges, and providing customers with coupons that build loyalty. While I just scratched the surface, there are many other benefits to owning and operating an ATM if you own a retail store which I discuss in another chapter.

Placing an ATM in a Commercial Building

A commercial building is also a good location for an ATM, especially if it has a cafeteria or extra space in the building to sub-let. It might be likely that other machines have already been installed there, so it's best to inquire. If this isn't the case, you should not hesitate to get one installed.

Shopping malls, small strip centers, and parking lots can also be wonderful locations. Look for busy shopping centers that might be too small for a bank to deploy an ATM.

These are often good locations, and the easiest way to find out who to speak with is to find out who handles the leasing for the tenants. Almost any tenant would give you-the leasing manager's contact information.

Installing an ATM Where You Work

You can definitely install an ATM where you work. However, keep in mind that if people know you own the ATM, they may not like that you are making all of the money from the surcharge fee. All kidding aside, you want to ensure there is a need for it and you don't hide the ATM in the break room.

If there are hundreds of employees, that would justify the need for an ATM. Suppose the company where you work only has 50 to 100 employees and there is no cafeteria or a place to spend money. In that case, coworkers may not need to spend $2.00 or $3.00 for convenience if there isn't a place nearby to spend it. Sure, on paydays, you may get a bunch of transactions, but if that's only two times a month, you aren't going to make a killing. Granted, you can always move the ATM somewhere else, but I'd suggest speaking to an experienced service provider to help you navigate a deal like this.

Installing an ATM in a Condo Complex

Yes, you can install an ATM in a condo complex. There are no restrictions on where you can install an ATM machine. However, you will need to get HOA approval if this is required.

A condo complex may not be an ideal location in many situations due to few potential customers. You cannot expect too much business if you install an ATM in a complex with only a few condos. An average of three transactions a day is what I look for as the bare minimum to have a decent ROI. Granted, 2 per day is still 60 transactions which at $3 is $180, and that's still a great ROI if you're not loading much cash, but I personally like busier locations, and they are out there if you look for them.

As always, if you're just starting out, discuss any potential locations with your chosen ATM company or processing provider. Be sure you speak with someone who has been in the business a long time and who personally operates ATMs daily. You want to learn and get opinions from someone with vast experience so you can learn from them and not make the same mistakes as opposed to getting advice from someone who has only been doing it a short time or who doesn't have experience with all types of scenarios.

Revenue Split

Setting up an ATM in someone else's store can often mean that you compensate the store owner for the use of the space. You can think of it like rent, but often enough, it's more like a revenue share or split deal. Whatever compensation or rent you agree on will be the monthly expense for the location. You'll have to calculate that into your projected revenues and costs.

It is a given that you have to pay the store owner something for the space the ATM occupies. However, the location owner also benefits. Around 30% of the cash withdrawn from ATMs located in stores is spent in that store. This means that the store's sales should get a boost from the ATM being installed there. Moreover, if the location accepts credit cards, its credit card acceptance will be offset by ATM usage, thus lowering credit card processing fees. I've even seen some locations abandon credit card acceptance once an ATM was installed.

Since you are operating an ATM business, it's best to collaborate with the store owner to ensure it's a win-win for you both. After all, if your business is new, it could take some time to establish a few good clients for a referral list. Setting up your machine in a well-known store will not only give your business credibility but will give you exposure and earn you and the store owner profits.

The best way to strike a deal with the store owner is to share the revenue. This way, it becomes a partnership or co-op, and you can also split responsibilities with the store owner. While just a few things need to be taken care of when operating an ATM machine, someone needs to do them. The tasks include loading cash (the vaulter), loading receipt paper, and other miscellaneous tasks like cleaning the machine and taking care of any errors like cash jams, paper jams, or card reader errors (although rare, they need to be addressed).

The revenue-sharing agreement often depends on the type of store where you plan to place your ATM. For instance, a retail store does not attract as many transactions as a casino. Therefore, the surcharge applied to ATMs in retail stores may need to be increased to meet the profit-sharing expectations of both parties. It's best to have some revenue projections to make the best decision when offering the store owner part of the revenue.

One thing you do need to consider is whether or not the store owner is bearing any costs related to the ATM. For instance, the store owner may agree to run the communication line via an internet connection which is an expense in and of itself. Although, I suggest a wireless device so you aren't tied to their ISP outages or issues.

Just make sure there are no surprises for the location owner. No one likes surprises, so be sure to discuss each party's responsibilities and put it all in a site location agreement before you install the machine. This will ensure that you keep operating the ATM in the store for a long time. I typically offer the location a share of the surcharge after the first 50 transactions so I can at least cover my expenses. The first 50 transactions at $3.00 help defray some banking fees, fuel and vehicle maintenance, travel time, and of course, equipment and maintenance. When negotiating the share, keep your costs in mind. You don't want regrets, and every deal needs to be a win-win.

Site Location Agreement (SLA)

Once you have verbal approval from the owner to place your ATM in his or her store, you need to obtain it in writing. We know some IADs who don't use an SLA, and that's just asking for trouble. Some store owners are casual, saying they don't need an agreement, but trust me, you want one. An SLA outlines the responsibilities and shows that you own and operate the ATM inside the location should there be any concern or issue where you need that proof. One example is when we had an ATM in a local eatery, and they went bankrupt without us knowing. We went to load cash one day, and the place was boarded up. Our machine still had a few hundred bucks in it, and we couldn't access it. We contacted the landlord, and since the restaurateur owed them rent, the landlord tried to claim the ATM was his. Luckily, our SLA proved otherwise, and we didn't have to take the landlord to small claims. He realized his error and let us in. The SLA is a simple agreement that is also your insurance policy in the event of unexpected circumstances. This is why the site location agreement has to be completed.

The site location agreement is a document that lists the terms and conditions between the two parties, i.e., you and the store owner. Though the deal depends on the things agreed upon between you and the store owner, there is a standard format you can follow. It usually lists a few clauses about your machine being installed in a retail store.

Again, and most importantly, the site location agreement clarifies that you are the owner of the ATM, and the store is listed as the location. Other details included in the site location agreement are:

- placement of the machine
- responsibilities to be borne by each party
- the length of time the deal is valid for
- insurance, maintenance, and other related issues

The site location agreement lists any relevant terms and conditions agreed upon by the two parties. To put it simply, the site location agreement defines the roles and responsibilities of the store owner and you, the operator of the ATM machine. Make sure you discuss all of the details of the agreement before signing on the dotted line. Be sure to ask your ATM provider if they offer an SLA template you can alter. In the resource section of this book, I'll share where to find the template I use, as well as other forms and help videos.

How to Talk to Location Owners and Negotiate a Deal

Back when I was going door-to-door selling ATMs before placements were popular, I would walk into a liquor store, convenience store, or small grocery store with a piece of plywood I painted black and cut to the exact dimensions as the base of the ATM. This way, I knew exactly how much space I would need without breaking out a tape measure.

I used to photocopy five $100 bills and tape them to one side of the plywood. I would walk through the store and find a spot where I thought the ATM could do well. Then, I would place the painted plywood on the floor with the $100 bills facing up.

When the person behind the counter wasn't busy, I would ask if the store owner or a manager was available. Typically, the answer would be, "Why?" Sometimes, the cashier would just say, "No." Even if they didn't ask why or if they said no, I would launch into my pitch and say I found $500 on the floor "over there" or "back there" and point to where I put the wood on the ground and wanted to show the owner or manager. This resulted in many different responses:

The cashier wouldn't believe me and would ask where I found the money. Then I'd say that I'd prefer to show the manager or owner and ask if they were the owner or manager. If not, I'd say that I'd like to call the owner personally. If I couldn't get the owner's phone number, I would give the cashier my phone number asking him or her to have the owner call me. Often, the owner did contact me. However, I would explain that I didn't have time to talk but would like to call back later or tomorrow so I could get their phone number (this part isn't necessary now because of caller ID). Now we just confirm their number before hanging up. The owner's contact information would then go into my sales call schedule so that I could try to make an in-person appointment.

In an alternative scenario, if the owner were at the store, I would introduce myself and get his or her name. Then I would show the owner the plywood on the floor with the photocopied $500. At first, owners thought I was trying to fool them, but since it was actually a sales gimmick, I had to quickly transition into my pitch.

I would say something like, "If you have just a few minutes, I want to show you how I can find $500 or more here every month just using this amount of space. Would you like to get $500 a month from this space?"

Most owners would be curious at that point. Very few said, "No, I already have plans for that space." If the owner expressed interest, I would ask for five to ten minutes to talk privately or make an appointment for a better time. I also had ATM brochures, a brief presentation, and my agreements on hand in case the owner wanted to learn more right then and there. Sometimes it was that easy to close the deal. Other times it took a few visits.

If my presentation left the owner unsure or uninterested, I would ask if he or she owned any other locations or knew anyone who could benefit from an on-site ATM. If, on the other hand, I closed the deal, I would get the appropriate paperwork in order to get the deal closed and follow up in a few days to make sure power and communication lines were ready. Once they were, I would visit again to check and schedule the delivery and installation.

Remember that back then, I was selling ATMs for hundreds of dollars per month on a five-year business lease. Today, you're not selling the owner anything. You want to try to place your own ATM in the location. This way, you remove the owner's risk and offer a reward. These days when you place an ATM, it's not going to make the merchant owners $500 per month. Still, if it's a good location, they could make at least $100 from the ATM transactions, experience incremental sales from the extra cash in the customers' hands, and save on credit card transaction fees. Since the ATM converts some customers from credit cards to cash, it reduces the merchant's credit card processing charges. You can explain this to the merchant: "On average, an ATM converts 10% - 20% of your credit card customers to cash customers. I'm sure you would prefer more cash sales, and if the ATM can save you just $5,000 to $10,000 in credit card receipts monthly, that should equate to saving at least another $100 - $200 or more a month in your pocket instead of paying that to your credit card processor." In other words, the location owners you speak to have nothing to lose by sharing their space with you.

It's essential to ensure your proposal is a win-win for you and the location owner. You want to negotiate favorable terms and conditions for all involved parties. Since the store owners are providing you with the space to install your ATM, they might expect a larger share of the revenue without taking on any responsibilities. But never make a deal where both parties—you and the store owner—are not completely happy. No matter how badly you may want that location, there are other opportunities if you can't strike a fair and equitable deal.

This is why you need to know how to negotiate with location owners. In this regard, your ATM provider can help you. I've added some info in the resources section about how I offer this help should you need it.

ATM providers have the experience of installing hundreds of machines before they install yours. As a result, they can help you to get the best terms and conditions that suit your needs. You should use their experience and expertise to get the terms you want. Any ATM provider not interested in helping you succeed isn't your ATM business partner. Look for an ATM provider that's interested in your success.

However, make sure you don't overdo the negotiation phase. Don't get carried away in the process and try to get everything in your favor. You have to allow some leeway to ensure the store owner doesn't lose interest in and cancel the agreement. If you ensure both parties can make money, everyone feels good about it, and the deal works for everyone, you will have a long and prosperous relationship. And you can ask for referrals. Word of mouth is the best advertising.

If you have some experience negotiating terms with locations, try it. If you don't have any experience, be sure to finish reading this book. It will help you find your footing in the ATM business. You don't need experience negotiating with locations; learning as you go is okay. The worst thing the location owner can do is say, "No." Each subsequent try will get you closer to a deal. Should you need it, I've included information on where to find telephone scripts with answers and objections at the end of this book. Check out the resources section at the end of this book for more information on telephone scripts you can use to help you with this part.

Where to Start

- People you already know who might have a good location
- New business listings
- Neighborhood establishments you already frequent

Start by talking to people you know who might have or know a good location. Talk to retailers you know or friends who might know of a good location for an ATM. You can also call new business listings to make appointments. There are many promising new business directories and listing resources such as publications and lists you can purchase. You can also use Yelp and Google Maps to create prospect lists and get the names and phone numbers from Searchbug.com.

If you are a frequent patron of an establishment you think would be a good place for your ATM, talk to the owner.

What to Do

- Approach location owners from a problem-solving perspective
- Offer a solution
- Ask for the owner's contact information

- Arrange an appointment
- Present SLA
- Close the deal

Remember, no one likes a sales pitch. It's much easier to approach location owners from a problem-solving perspective. State a problem many retailers have and offer your solution. For example, one main problem for most retailers is the cost of accepting credit cards. If you are buying something with your credit card in the store, make a friendly comment that accepting credit cards is getting more expensive and complicated. Then listen to what the other person says.

You can then let them know that you're in the business of placing free ATMs in local stores that qualify. You might need to reiterate that you are not in the merchant processing business (unless you are), and you're not selling anything. You help small business owners reduce their credit card fees at no cost, and you can explain it in just a few minutes. Then ask for the owner's contact information so you can pass that information along.

Most of the time, if you come off as humble and nice, that should get you the owner's name and phone number. Be sure to get the name of the person who gave you the contact information, too, so you can use it when you call the owner.

Another approach is to casually ask if there is an ATM close by, and then ask if other customers ask about an ATM. Depending on the answer, ask for the owner's contact information. Say that you offer ATM solutions for free.

If the employee is hesitant to give you that information, ask if a manager is available or ask for a good time to visit when the owner is on-site. The key to this visit is to get the contact info for the decision maker so you can talk to him or her to see if there is any interest in having an ATM in the store.

When you do reach the decision maker, be sure to let him or her know you are a frequent customer. Explain that the employee you spoke with mentioned that customers often ask if an ATM is available or nearby. Then ask if he or she has ever considered adding an ATM to the establishment, especially if customers are sent across the street or down the block to another business to access this service.

Be sure to approach the owner or manager as a patron or business person, not a salesperson. Let owners know you're a frequent shopper and like their businesses. Don't make it a casual conversation if you get the opportunity to speak to them in person. Be sure to have a pen and paper or your smartphone handy to collect the owner's contact information so you can schedule a mutually convenient time to meet and sit down to explain all the details.

You can let the owner know you help businesses get ATMs for free and would be interested in putting one in his or her business at no cost. Depending on the level of interest, you can even show where you think a good location for the ATM is. (Obviously, before you do that, make sure you have already scoped out the premises and have a good idea of the location for an ATM placement.)

Let the owner know that all you need is one square foot of floor space (it's a little more than that); don't go into too many details.

At any point, if the owner is interested when you are first talking, or if you are speaking over the phone, offer to meet with him or her to discuss the opportunity at a mutually convenient time in his or her office. Ask if mornings, afternoons, or evenings are the best time to meet. Then make an actual appointment. Do not go into too many details on the phone. The phone is only to get a face-to-face meeting. It is much easier for anyone to say no thanks over the phone or not listen since they didn't initiate the call. An in-person meeting at a mutually agreed-upon time will get you much farther.

Once you have a firm appointment and the owner's undivided attention, you will know whether he or she is seriously interested. Then you can talk about the details. Include how the owner will make more money by having an ATM. Explain that it can lower credit card costs, increase impulse spending, and add a small share of the surcharge. (You can start with $0.50 or $1.00 after the first 50 transactions or anything you want.) Be prepared with an SLA and close the deal.

Locations That Have a Liquor License

Installing an ATM machine in a liquor store or any other adult location where liquor is served is typically a great location. Note that some states have passed legislation restricting the use of Electronic Benefits Transfer (EBT) cards in ATMs in liquor stores. EBT is the government welfare network. If you get government assistance, your debit card uses the EBT network and won't allow transactions in some of these locations. This is not necessarily a bad thing since most EBT cards can't be surcharged anyway. But if the liquor store owner asks, you must know this information.

Installing an ATM in a liquor store will prove to be quite lucrative. Generally, ATM businesses can place a higher surcharge fee on ATMs installed in liquor stores or establishments serving liquor since the higher cost can be justified by the convenience. There is a good chance that your

ATM will see a considerable number of customers here, mainly if you have selected the liquor store carefully.

I've also seen more transactions in liquor stores in undesirable neighborhoods if the machine dispenses $10s instead of $20s. When calculating the estimated number of daily customers, if the store is in a restrictive welfare state, be sure to ask the owner for his estimate on how many of those patrons are on government assistance. This way, you can back those out of your calculations.

Locations Going Through Change of Ownership

Generally, SLAs are drawn up for an effective period of three to five years. Some store owners don't like long agreements; however, as the ATM owner, you want the longest possible term for your agreements, as you certainly don't want to have to remove your ATM if it's making money or, worse, is proving to be such a great business that the store owner purchases his or her own ATM from a competitor. The longer the SLA term, the better it is for you so that if the store owner does sell the location and isn't just moving to a bigger or better location, you could have the right to transfer the SLA to the new owner so you won't have to remove the ATM.

There is, however, a chance that the business owner could relocate or sell the store before the end of your agreement. What happens, then? If the owner relocates to, perhaps, expand the store or get a better location, and you've established a good relationship, then you will most likely follow to the new location. That is the easiest thing to do.

However, it may not be feasible if the owner moves farther away than you're willing to travel. Also, the business might be shutting down for good. In either case, you are the one who has to relocate and bear the hassles and costs associated with the move. If the owner sells the location, your SLA should have a provision that transfers rights to the new owner. Ensure the previous owner introduces you to the new owner and helps you transition if the store is being sold.

This is why it is good you discuss the business's future plans (how long they have been in the same location or how long is left on the lease) with the owner when creating the SLA. If the owner plans to move soon, it may or may not be a good idea for you to install a machine there.

Even if the business doesn't plan to relocate but has to because of other circumstances, the SLA should state that the machine's owner (you) be notified well in advance. Generally speaking, the location should inform you at least thirty days before the intended move. You can also negotiate and get the store owner to increase the notice period so that you know about the relocation a little earlier.

In the case of a change of ownership, you can contact the new owner to discover whether or not he or she would be interested in having an ATM on the premises. Since the machine has already been installed and people know about it, the business owner has nothing to lose from continuing to have it there. In that case, you are in luck, as you don't have to move the machine from one place to another.

However, suppose the new owner is not interested in an ATM machine being there. In that case, you may end up having to relocate. Again, the SLA will guide you as to the responsibilities of the previous location in such a case. You can negotiate to have the cost of relocation included in the SLA. I suggest you negotiate a split or flat rate fee if forced to move through no fault of your own. While that is ideal, don't let that be the deal breaker in a location you think will do well. Moving the machine isn't a big deal; it's best to get it running for a few years rather than not at all.

ORDERING AN ATM MACHINE

Now that you know the paperwork and documentation involved in placing an order for an ATM and how to secure a location, it's time to learn how to actually place the order.

How to Order An ATM

You can order an ATM machine from a reputable ATM provider. ATM providers are well-versed in the paperwork and other formalities necessary to complete your order. However, there are some decisions you will have to make before you place the order.

First, you need to know how you will pay for the machine. Will you use a check or credit card to buy the machine outright, lease, get a loan, or ask about creative financing? If you're ordering an ATM online without speaking to anyone, you would typically use a credit card. While some ATM providers accept credit card payments to purchase the machine, others don't. Some providers may accept payments over a short term if you plan to process transactions with them after you have a track record. Some providers will also offer low-cost leasing as well as loans. Loans are typically for $10K and up, so a loan is worth looking into if you plan to purchase four to six machines, but many IADs finance ATM purchases with no-interest credit card offers. You know, the ones that let you charge or transfer for 12-18 months with zero interest. If you go this route, be sure to save enough surcharge revenue to pay down the card balance by the due date to avoid a shock when it comes due.

Furthermore, you must decide whether you want to buy a new or refurbished machine (if available). In either case, talk to your ATM provider. They can help you select the best machine for your location, ensure that the order is placed correctly, and get the machine delivered in the shortest possible time.

Find a reliable ATM provider and get the ATM machine you want. It's as simple as placing an online order, completing an equipment order form, or using your ISO or Sub-ISO mobile app or electronic forms.

Shipping

New machines are usually shipped directly from the manufacturer's location. This guarantees that the machine you are purchasing has a recent manufacturer's date (which you can verify from a decal inside the top of the ATM), is updated with all ADA requirements (more on this in a later chapter), and has all of the current and necessary network security requirements.

In the case of refurbished ATMs, sometimes the processing partner or your ATM provider will ship the machine. This is because the machine has to be cleaned, tested, and programmed for installation. You also want to make sure it is a model that can still process transactions on the networks. (If you get a refurbished ATM from anywhere else, there is no guarantee it will work with your provider.)

Regardless of who ships the machine, the address you provide when you order should be where you want the ATM shipped. Unless you have an easy method to transport the ATM, it's always best to send the machine to where it will be installed.

EQUIPMENT OPTIONS

Before there were ATMs, there were scrip machines. Scrip machines allowed users to swipe their cards, enter their PINs, and select a dollar amount. The machine produced a receipt the user gave to the merchant as a voucher used to pay for goods and receive cash back. It could only be redeemed at that location.

Scrip machines were great for locations where ATMs didn't perform well enough to justify the cost, i.e., locations with little traffic. Store owners liked scrip machines because they took up little space, cost less than an ATM, required only a phone line for setup, didn't store cash, sped up checkout processes, reduced credit card processing fees, encouraged in-store and impulse purchases, and brought in revenue in the form of surcharge, expired credit, and unused or unclaimed credit.

Additionally, modern scrip machines are now point-of-sale (POS) transactions rather than ATM transactions. This means that the limits imposed by banks on bank cards don't apply. This is good news for casinos and other locations encouraging high cash transactions.

Scrip machines and ATMs are very similar in function and share many of the same benefits. The most significant advantage is that they help stores and other businesses avoid credit card processing fees. When merchants process a credit card transaction, they must pay a percentage to the credit card processing company. By encouraging cash payments, businesses lower their credit card fees.

Scrip machines are rare these days, and most are long gone. ATMs take their place.

You want to find locations that experience a lot of traffic to justify a surcharge high enough to get the ROI as quickly as possible. Therefore, to ensure the success of your ATM business, you'll want to invest in high-quality ATM machines with the biggest screen you can afford. There is no dearth of options when it comes to buying ATM machines, which is both good and bad.

The good thing is that you have plenty of options to choose from, ensuring you can get precisely what you are looking for. The bad thing is that you can feel confused and make the wrong choice with such a variety to explore. When starting your ATM business, the last thing you would want is to select a substandard machine. The best option is to stick to the best machines with the largest, most attractive screen available at the time. We are all glued to screens. Cell phone screens are getting bigger, and for an ATM to get the attention of users, it has to be bigger than their cell phones. Remember when people started seeing the screens in a Tesla? Everyone was talking about them. Yeah, most people, when talking about a Tesla the first time, almost always mentioned it: "Did you see the size of the screen?" Okay, so get the best bang for your buck when it comes to ATMs, but screen size should be the first consideration.

I've highlighted a few of them below.

When choosing ATM equipment, you want to select the option that's best for you personally. I can provide you with a list of recommendations based on my experience in the industry. Still, only you know what amount of space and budget you have to work with. Those are factors to consider when shopping for a machine.

Machine Types

You first want to consider the type of ATM machine you want. Your options are free-standing, through-the-wall (TTW), and wall mount.

MACHINE TYPES

  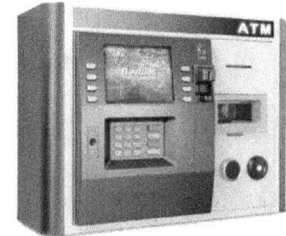

FREE-STANDING   THROUGH-THE-WALL   WALL MOUNT

Free-standing ATM machines are the most common because they are easier to place. They can be placed anywhere there is a power supply, giving you more freedom to move them around and find the most optimal location in the store or business.

TTW ATM machines are larger and heavier than free-standing ATMs. This is because the back half of the machine (the interface) goes into, or through, a wall that protrudes into another room. Suppose this space already exists at your location. In that case, a TTW ATM is beneficial because you can more safely access the vault behind closed doors. TTW ATMs are the most secure because a room with controlled access protects them. If this space doesn't exist but you like the idea of the added security, it will take a little construction work to create a hole in the wall to insert your TTW ATM. You might also consider a TTW ATM if you want the front (chassis) to face outside, allowing 24/7 access for customers to use the machine even outside of store or business hours. These are great for parking lots or where you see a vacant kiosk.

A wall-mount ATM is the smallest option. These work best at locations with little space to work with and little traffic. They can conveniently be mounted to a wall, table, or counter. This smaller machine will hold fewer notes than the other two, so if your location is busy, you might want a larger machine to ensure you don't run out of cash throughout the day.

The machine type you purchase will depend heavily on your available space.

My Current Favorites

Hyosung

Hyosung is a leading provider of ATM hardware, software, and service. Their ATM machines are reliable, durable, and flexible.

The Hyosung Halo II is a free-standing machine named because of the "halo" of LED lighting surrounding the keypad. This feature draws customers in and is ideal for dimly lit locations like bars and restaurants. Surprisingly, some bar employees can get annoyed with the Halo flashing, so it's best to know the surroundings and keep the color change mode to a minimum if the Halo is within view of an employee that has to constantly see it changing colors. Depending on the venue, a solid color or non-flashing mode could be more appropriate.

However, this is perhaps the one ATM machine that can attract passersby and get them to withdraw cash without the biggest screen. Needless to say, many ATM businesses using Hyosung Halo II (2600 SE) ATMs are more successful than others when using this feature. The lights in the Halo can be configured in various ways and colors depending upon your needs and the location atmosphere.

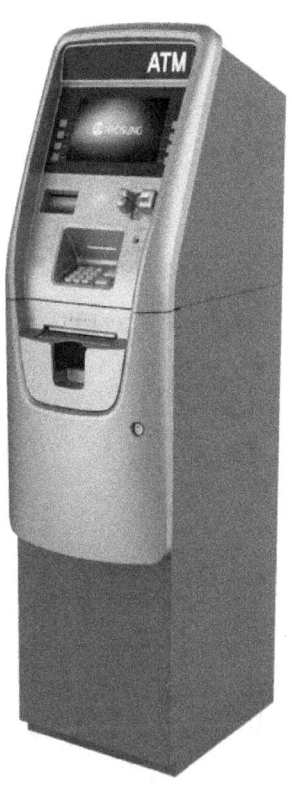

The "halo" is attractive, and the machine has a 10-inch LCD screen, which is also quite captivating. The screen can be optimized to add graphics. The Hyosung Halo II ATM's operating system is Windows, a proven mainstream standard for ATMs. Be wary of any ATM that is running proprietary operating systems these days.

Genmega

Genmega is another leader in the industry with a reputation for cutting-edge engineering and integration. The Genmega Onyx-W is a wall-mount or countertop ATM. While it's a compact footprint (19.7" H x 26.8" W x 10.4" D) and a weight of only 121 lbs, this ATM still packs a punch with a 10.1" screen and other great features.

The G2500 is a free-standing option similar to the Halo II and almost as popular. It has an 8″ TFT high-resolution 32-bit color LCD screen. The Genmega G2500 is the least expensive Genmega ATM machine. All Genmega ATMs come standard with the GenCam, a camera that takes a photo of the customer, which is handy for dispute resolution.

The Genmega G2500 pictured below with a shark skip wrap is a machine you should consider if you intend to set up an ATM at a busy location. This ATM's unique aspect is the option to install one, two, or four cassettes. This allows ATM operators to load a considerable amount of cash into the machine for fewer trips, accommodate really busy locations, and load multiple denominations. Even with constant withdrawals, this machine doesn't run out of cash quickly. This is a great option for professional vaulting or multiple cassettes in a traditional environment.

Multiple cassettes make the machine easier to operate since you don't have to reload the cassette as often. Still, the price difference may or may not be worthwhile. You would have to factor in all the associated costs, including travel to the ATM, to see if the numbers come out in your favor. Remember that you can space out your visits to the ATM location if you load it yourself. Instead of going once a week for a single cassette machine, you may go once or twice a month. The capability to hold multiple cassettes also means that the machine can be programmed to dispense different denominations like $20s and $5s if you have two cassettes. This allows for many different combinations of withdrawal, a feature some customers appreciate.

The Onyx and Nova ATMs can future-proof your business with their updated design but come at an increased cost. The G2500 still looks very much like the modern ATM machine that it is, while newer models are starting to look futuristic. While this machine typically comes standard with an 8-inch color LCD screen with a high-resolution display, I recommend an upgrade to the 10.2" touch screen, making it look and feel very professional, which will stand the test of time better than an 8" screen which is only slightly larger than some of the big cell phones and smaller than many tablets. A 10" to 12" screen is closer to the size of a tablet many customers are used to. So, seeing a big screen evokes a comfort level they are accustomed to. The G2500 is a great ATM to offer locations with older machines if you want to try and get the account.

The Onyx is a step above the G2500, offering a standard 10.1" screen with an optional 12" touchscreen upgrade; the 12" upgrade is a beautiful sight. This ATM is also available with an optional bill-presenting mechanism that dispenses the bills in a bundle for the customer. Most retail ATMs only have a spray dispenser, which dispenses bills individually into a tray. A bill presenter is unnecessary, but this machine is for high-end locations where you might charge a percentage of the withdrawal amount or where a high-end ATM is required to get the account, like in a casino or other high-volume venue. It also looks very impressive in a dispensary. This is also helpful at busy events, so you avoid long wait times, and people don't get frustrated waiting in line.

Triton

Triton has been a market leader since the 90s. They are the only ATM manufacturer to say their ATMs are made in the USA. In 1992 they formed the Original Triton Systems' Advisory Committee, of which I was one of the first five members for a 2-year seat.

Triton is one of the ATM manufacturers and still produces quality machines. Their ARGO line is a little more expensive than other manufacturers. If you work with the financial industry, check out the ARGO line of ATMs if you need a top-of-the-line ATM to work with a bank or other financial business.

The Triton Rl600 and RL2000 series ATMs are tried and true retail machines, but they are only available used or refurbished. However, with the new keypad requirements starting in 2025, all the keypads in these machines will need to be upgraded to the T10 design. Any new ATMs should already have the new T10, so make sure that no matter whom you buy an ATM from, it's not old inventory. The older 9600 and 9100 series machines have been discontinued.

New vs. Refurbished

All ATMs in the United States must be EMV-enabled. If you purchase a used ATM without EMV capabilities, you might be able to upgrade an existing card reader, but it may be difficult since they are considered ancient now. Ensure an EMV kit is installed or available for any older ATM before buying one, and make sure it can accommodate the upgraded T10 keypads that will be mandatory starting in 2025;

otherwise, you will be buying a boat anchor. There are ATMs that can't be used any longer as the hardware can't support the latest software or network standards. Be careful when buying older used equipment. Stick with a manufacturer date after 2018 to be better, safe than sorry if buying used machines.

When buying used, you also want to ask if the machine has been refurbished. Refurbished means that the ATM hasn't just been cleaned; it has been retrofitted with any required hardware upgrades, has the newest software upgrades, and is furnished with replacement decals before being sold. Used parts should be fixed or replaced, making a refurbished machine nicer than a used machine.

I recommend ordering a new ATM as your first ATM machine so you have the smoothest introduction to the business. Used machines add complications. Technology improves with newer machines making them easier to use with updated graphics, input functionalities, bigger screens, and more straightforward operator menus.

I like the Hyosung Halo II, Force, or Genmega brands for new ATMs, but you can get refurbished Tritons for a little less. I just don't think it's worth saving $500 - $800 if the ATM is going to look vintage in a few years. Since ATM models can change, I won't go into too many more details. Suffice it to say that you can research new ATM models online. I also added a few links to some of my favorite new machines in the resources section if you'd like to explore your options.

There is a host of upgrades and optional hardware you can also purchase for an ATM machine. Most ATMs are not heavy, weighing around 150 - 225 lbs, but the overall size is typically small. They can fit nicely into tight spaces and don't use much room where floor space is precious. Plus, they are incredibly durable. Equipment prices will fluctuate, so you will want to contact your ATM provider for up-to-date pricing on any ATM models. However, at the time of publication, you should be able to get a machine configured nicely with a decent size screen, an electronic lock, and delivery for about $2,500 - $3,000.

Machines to Avoid

With so many new Americans with Disabilities Act (ADA) requirements, new network regulations, hacking, and encryption tools over the last few years, an abundance of used or outdated ATMs have shown up on the used market and will continue to do so. Unfortunately, these are typically purchased by unsuspecting new ATM operators looking for a deal, and they get duped.

These old ATMs (maybe not as old as the Tidel Anycard ATMs I sold; picture from 1994) are nothing but boat anchors or spare parts for dying models. Many of these ATMs can't even legally be run in the United States any longer.

Some of these ATMs include older or vintage ATM models by Tidel, Triton, and Hantle. Ensure the manufactured date of any ATM you look at is less than five to six years old if you want to future-proof yourself. Don't buy any ATMs that are over five years old. Stay away from Tidel, Diebold, and NCR ATMs, as they can be problematic and non-compliant. While Triton ATMs are wonderful, they have been around a long time, so many outdated ones appear on auction sites. If you are considering a used Triton, find out the model and the year it was manufactured. Many Triton ATMs can no longer be upgraded, and many older models have been retired and can no longer run on the networks since they are now out of compliance. Speak with your ATM company about processing any older machines before you buy one.

All ATMs have a manufactured date. If the ATM was manufactured before 2012, it probably won't even comply with ADA standards. Then, by the time you pay for the ATM, ship it, and try to find parts to refurbish or upgrade it, you could have purchased a new ATM with a parts and labor warranty for around the same amount. When unsure, please call your ATM company.

OPTIONAL HARDWARE

Regarding optional hardware you can buy for your ATM machines, a topper, an e-lock, and a wireless device are the foremost among them.

Topper

A topper is a type of screen or light installed on the ATM machine that displays video or is just a translucent backlit panel with the letters "ATM." Alternatively, you can go to a sign shop or make arrangements with your ATM provider to get custom inserts for the toppers with your logo and phone number if you'd like. Still, it's really meant to draw people to the ATM.

Toppers are also a way you can use your machines for marketing. The sign and/or video on the topper can be used for many things. There was a time when ATM business owners had to think twice before investing in a topper. The equipment was expensive, and the concept of ATM-based marketing wasn't popular. Now, toppers sometimes pay for themselves.

Technological improvements have significantly decreased the cost of purchasing an ATM topper. This means you can easily buy a topper for your machines, sell advertising, or lease the space to advertising companies if you have enough real estate. Also, people have begun to expect more from ATMs. Installing a topper allows you to capture their attention and fulfill their expectations.

Most importantly, you can use the topper screen for marketing. This is particularly helpful if you have installed your machine in a retail establishment. You will find it easier to retain and attract customers when you have a topper screen displaying offers and incentives.

The technology used in ATM screens is now at the level where ATM businesses can make the most out of topper screens. Therefore, when you order an ATM machine, ask the provider if they also offer topper screens or if they recommend one for the location where you're installing it. Toppers rarely come pre-installed. They typically ship separately and are an easy field install. If you hire or pay for professional installation, installing the topper is typically included. Otherwise, it's a very straightforward DIY job. There are third-party media companies that specialize in ATM toppers (see resources section for more information). Using a specialized media company is easier unless you are familiar with selling ad space. This is an additional revenue stream once you have enough real estate (the space on top of the ATM in enough establishments). Speak with your ATM provider regarding any experience they might have if they have worked with any ATM media vendors or if they found it profitable for them. I have had some good and some not-so-great experiences with toppers. If you have 20 or more locations, it can be worth pursuing, but they don't produce a ton of revenue unless you sell the ad space yourself.

Despite its various benefits, a video or illuminated topper (aka high topper) remains a hardware option. They aren't inexpensive, so you need to ensure you can ROI a topper, and some locations may want them or require more space for them. If you plan to install a topper of any size as an additional component, get the measurements and plan appropriately. Note any height restrictions where you are installing the ATM. Also, ensure the location owner knows about the topper and that you have the right to sell the topper ad space in your SLA. The last thing you want is to go through the trouble of arranging a video topper and advertising only to have the location owner upset about it due to unmanaged expectations.

E-Lock

An e-lock is an electronic lock for the safety of the ATM. Many ATMs come standard with a regular dial combination safe lock. You know the type: three to the right, two to the left, one to the right until it opens. If you plan to load several machines at a time or would like quick and easy access, upgrading to an e-lock is a no-brainer. You'll save hours of safe opening over the life of the machine. Depending on the type, ordering a new ATM typically costs $50-$100 extra for this upgrade. If you wait to order it and want to do an e-lock upgrade in the field, it will be a lot more expensive.

Mas Hamilton Lock

A Mas Hamilton (now Kaba Mas or Cencon) lock is an upgraded lock most armored carriers require. If you plan to have your ATM loaded by an armored carrier, this lock ensures that the opening and closing of the ATM are tracked for auditing. It requires special keys and computer software for the tracking of every entry. Each key is coded to the person opening the safe. The only reason to get this lock is if your vaulting vendor requires it. Talk to your ATM company for further details if you need this service. These locks are a lot more expensive than any other lock.

Wireless Devices

There are two ways you can connect your ATM to your ATM processor to communicate transactions:

1. Use the location's internet service (ISP).
2. Use a wireless router designed for ATM communications.

An ATM cellular modem, also known as an ATM wireless router, gives you full control over your ATM's communications. It uses secure encryption but sends the encrypted signal over cell phone networks. The data packets are so small and compressed with encryption that the monthly fee for ATM transactions is typically less 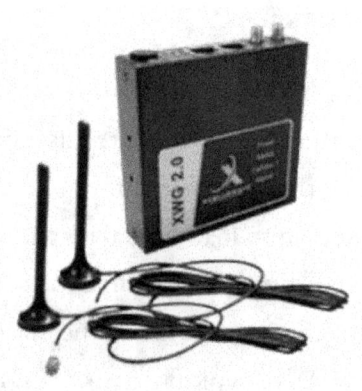 than the cost of the standard old phone lines. Without it, you are at the mercy of the location's internet service provider. So if the location's router goes down, service is interrupted, the location owner fails to pay the bill on time, or their account has any issues, you lose money while that ATM machine is inoperable.

When setting up your machine, it is crucial that you ask the location owner if he or she has high-speed internet service (the key word is "high speed") so that you can have them add a hardwired RJ45 jack where you plan to place the ATM. However, honestly, I never use the merchant's ISP any longer. Wireless devices have a guarantee, are less expensive than the old phone lines, and typically allow for unlimited ATM transactions for a low monthly fee.

Over the years, I've experienced too many headaches not owning the communications for the ATM. Also, note that I recommend you get the ATM and the wireless device from the same vendor. Otherwise, they don't know whose responsibility it is when there is an issue and can point fingers at each other. When you purchase the ATM, wireless modem, and wireless service from the same provider, you get total support under one roof with the same support contact.

If you decide to use the location's internet service and their ISP goes down or they have communication problems due to hardware, your ATM will be out of service until they fix it. Another con to using the location's ISP is "bad actors." Upset customers or former employees have been known to unplug the RJ45 cable if it's not hidden. So, if you're using the location's ISP, be on site when they install it so that you can be sure it is directly behind the ATM for the best security. You don't want to make unnecessary visits just to plug it back in later.

Also, retail locations aren't typically tech-savvy. Their ISP modems and routers are often stuck in an obscure area or a closet that doesn't get much ventilation or cleaning. ISP modems and routers are not infinitely reliable. If you plan to forgo a wireless device, it'll save you a few bucks a month. However, it's not *if* it's *when* you have communication problems using the retailer's ISP; you'll remember reading this. Just be prepared to get a wireless device at some point unless your ATM is in a franchise or chain store with someone managing IT functions.

If you go with the wireless communication option, you control it. All the equipment hides inside the ATM. I always go wireless. I've learned my lesson the hard way. If the retailer has really inexpensive service, an "off-name" provider, or DSL (usually slow and problematic), don't use it! It will be a massive headache down the road, and you'll need to get wireless service anyway. Wireless monthly costs are typically less than losing a few transactions, so it's cheap insurance to ensure good communications.

An ATM cellular modem also gives you more freedom regarding where to place your ATM machine. If there is no internet line near the perfect spot for your machine, you need a wireless device to utilize that space. This way, you aren't limited to areas with an internet jack if those spaces aren't optimal. You can still install your ATM machine with a wireless connection if your location isn't wired with ethernet. This allows you to place your machine anywhere with access to electrical power without hassle.

Wireless devices use 4G data connection from cellular networks. They will use 5G in the future with major carriers such as AT&T, Sprint, Verizon, and T-Mobile.

Some wireless providers require you to provide the zip code of your location to check for the carrier with the best signal in your area. Some wireless providers have multi-carrier SIMs, a smart card inside the wireless device with a unique identification number to recognize and transact with the ATM. The multi-carrier SIM will automatically change to the strongest carrier should there be interference from weather or damage to the default network. Removing it will prevent operation.

With a single carrier SIM option, if one particular carrier experiences spotty or unreliable cellular connection, you have to wait for coverage to ensue or have another SIM you can swap out.

Multi-carrier ATM cellular modems can be set up for mobile and event ATMs. Since the location of these ATMs will change frequently, multi-carrier modems accommodate any carrier. Hence, you guarantee you get the strongest connection no matter where you are. They are only a little more expensive but only sometimes necessary. Work with your ATM vendor to determine the best setup for your scenario.

With a wireless device, you can operate your ATM machine anywhere from a farmer's market to a concert as long as you have access to electrical power. When talking to your ATM service or wireless provider, ask them if they offer multi-carrier SIMs if you want the latest and greatest technology. Otherwise, you may need a new wireless modem if you move the ATM eventually and need a different wireless carrier.

There is an additional cost associated with purchasing a wireless device. At this time, wireless device costs are between $7.99 - $19.99 per month based on the wireless device hardware (which can be leased or purchased). Some providers offer the wireless modem to buy as a one-time purchase. Just make sure you know what router/modem you're getting. I like InHand routers that can handle a multi-carrier SIM.

Since a wireless device ensures that your ATM is always available to communicate with the host and avoids most potential communication problems that can occur using the location's ISP, you'll save both time and money. Wireless devices provide a host of benefits. First of all, transactions are much faster. Issues with local ISP communications can cause slow transaction processing times, intermittent transaction success, or wholly interrupted transactions. This frustrates users, location staff, and you. Second, you don't have to worry about losing connection or troubleshooting with the location owner, manager, or ISP. You own the end-to-end communication and can quickly handle any issues yourself. Third, you open yourself up to more placement options. You can also set up and get alerts from your wireless device. Finally, you can purchase a wireless device at any time. If you aren't sure whether or not you want or need one, or maybe you need some time to budget the cost, you can always add it later. Because the benefits heavily outweigh the cost, I highly recommend that anyone seriously operating an ATM business own the end-to-end communication using an ATM cellular modem to operate a wireless ATM.

EMV Card Reader

ATM/debit cards issued by financial institutions have had EMV chips for the past several years. Some are even doing away with the magnetic stripe entirely since it's no longer secure. <u>EMV chip card transactions</u> improve security against fraud compared to magnetic stripe card transactions. All new ATMs require and include chip readers.

Removable Cassette or Multiple Cassette Upgrade

Specific cassettes are an optional hardware upgrade. Several ATM machines come standard with a fixed note cassette. This means that you have to fill the ATM in place. You can't remove the cassette and take it into a back room to fill it. If you plan to load a large amount of cash, load cash during open hours or would like privacy while loading the money, I highly recommend you opt for a removable cassette or get an ATM that comes with one already.

Multiple-cassette ATMs are best suited for high-traffic locations or locations requiring more than one denomination. In multiple-cassette ATMs, you can load as many denominations as there are cassettes. In a 2-cassette ATM, you can load $10s and $20s, for example. Or, if your ATM is in a busy casino, you may want to load $20s and $100's. Just be sure you load the right cassettes with the proper denomination. I recommend labeling your cassettes with a denomination decal if you have more than one.

Surrounds, Wraps, and Decals

Surrounds and wraps are decorative options as opposed to hardware options. These can be handy in helping you beat out your competition. Hotels often require a surround; you can purchase a nice standard or custom wooden one online. Many standard surrounds are available for most ATM models, but most local cabinet shops can make a custom surround if necessary, and you'll avoid shipping fees and potential delivery damage. Your ATM provider will have a list of surround manufacturers they have worked with if you need one, but I find that talking to local cabinet makers often produces a nicer unit if your location requires one.

Wraps are typically thick graphic panels attached to the ATM. There are several brands. Have you ever seen a car, truck, bus, or other vehicle with pictures wrapped around the entire body? Well, you can do the same thing to an ATM machine, except the material is heavier, and anyone can apply them in the field without tools. With a custom graphic wrap, you can make your ATM look like anything you want. Pricing varies if you need it custom designed, but it's pretty reasonable, and there are many standard designs that look great. Ask your ATM company what's available if you want to make your ATM stand out with a surround or a wrap, and check the resource section for a recommended company.

Decals are a less expensive option and can be purchased from various online decal makers. I prefer inexpensive signage since they are easily replaced if you want to change them out. Plus, there are a lot of decal sign shops locally if you want something custom. My firm offers a variety of ATM decals and custom decals you can add on to almost any decal order.

ATM SCREENS

A majority of ATM business owners don't know the influence that the size and color of the ATM screens have on their business. Consequently, they don't pay much attention to the screen type they select when ordering equipment. So don't skip this chapter!

Color Screens

Modern ATMs come equipped with color screens regardless of the brand you purchase. It is a standard feature on most of today's ATMs since the price of LED and LCD panels has dropped. So you typically don't have to pay extra to get a color screen-equipped ATM. Most ATM business owners fail to make the most of the large color screens available on machines. There are numerous benefits of large color screens.

First, they add an eye-catching color image that captures the customers' attention. A store logo or custom welcome screen on your ATM is more professional and appealing to customers. In studies that I've done, ATMs with a color welcome screen experience higher usage. People feel more connected when the image on the ATM looks like the surroundings or instills confidence about using your ATM. This is particularly true of individuals who spend most of their time in the vicinity and are likely to use your machine regularly.

Another great benefit of color screens on your ATMs is that most modern ones have screens that rotate images like a slideshow. This means that you can add multiple images. The image will change at an interval you set (usually from five to thirty seconds), and a different image will appear at each interval. The best thing about the rotating screens is that they are eye-catching so that you can capture the attention of the people passing by your ATM.

You can have advertisement screens rotate with the welcome and transaction screens. It can be an ad for the machine's location, offering a special deal to ATM users, selling advertising space to local businesses, or even advertising your business to get more ATM locations.

You also have the opportunity to brand the machines you buy for your business by having your logo circulate on the welcome screen when the ATM is idle. This is a great way to signify your brand identity and show that your company operates the machine.

At the end of the day, it is up to you, the owner, to decide what you want to do with the color screen. Remember that you have a few possibilities to explore, so choose accordingly. Most ATM providers charge $95 per screen to create a custom welcome screen, but you can easily create one yourself. Your ATM provider should provide the specifications for this task for your ATM equipment type. A custom welcome screen is so important that my company offers them to every IAD on new purchases.

If you are the location owner and run your own ATM, ensure your ATM shows special offers or promotions on the screen. For instance, you may advertise your Happy Hour to passersby. In other words, the color screen will help educate your customers about your business. Many ATMs now have a 10" or 12" screen upgrade available, which is the size of an iPad or tablet. Hence, people are confident and comfortable using them. Smaller screens may seem antiquated, but it really depends on the area being used.

Huge screens make for an excellent presentation and can provide users and passersby with information so that they just might make a purchase.

As you can see, there are numerous benefits of color screens for an ATM business. Since color screens are a standard feature, there is no doubt that you will buy an ATM that already has a color screen. The primary purpose of highlighting these benefits is to inform you of how you can optimize them if you use them properly.

Screen Sizes

Apart from having a color screen on your machines, it is also essential that you know about the different screen sizes available. Only then can you choose the most appropriate size based on the type of customers you want to attract. When it comes to screen sizes, there are several, but three main options available to you are

1. 8" LCD (Hyosung and Triton) and 8" TFT LCD (Genmega)
2. 10.1-12.1" (Hyosung and Genmega)

All four brands mentioned here provide color screens. So, regardless of your screen size, you can buy ATMs with color screens. The prices of all these models vary but are typically comparable, as is the technology used. As of this writing, the biggest screen you can buy is 17" on the Nova or a TTW, but that may be overkill unless you have a great venue for a thru-the-wall or a high-volume location where you are competing for attention or need to attract attention from farther away.

The Hyosung Force has a 12.1" LCD screen. It is a popular option as it looks great with a custom ad screen. This machine also offers the opportunity to upgrade to the Monivision Camera, an option currently unavailable for the Halo II. This camera takes a snapshot of the customer while the PIN is entered and again when cash is dispensed. Users can see themselves on screen, which deters tampering, fraud, and theft. The images are also saved to the ATM journal to help ATM owners resolve customer disputes.

Genmega also offers a camera system. Genmega, however, includes the GenCam camera system on all their machines as a standard feature for no additional cost.

The current largest screen for a freestanding machine with a comparable price of all four brands listed is 12.1". You can upgrade the Genmega G2500 from the standard 8" screen to a 10.2" wide LCD touchscreen for only $250 as of this writing. Other models like the Genmega Onyx can be upgraded to a 12" screen and include the Gencam. The latest Genmega model, the Nova, comes standard with a 17" screen. The Hyosung Force comes standard with a 12.1" LCD screen.

While it can be confusing to determine the screen size you need, the general rule is to install the biggest screen you can afford. If you are going to install your ATM in a high-end nightclub or other venues that may not be well-lit or where your ATM will be competing for attention with flashing, colored dance lights or other forms of advertising, the larger and brighter the screen, the better. Keep your graphics bright and use whites, greens, and yellows in the images versus blacks, reds, and browns, as these tend to make the screen darker and harder to see.

Suppose you're installing the ATM in a rough area or a parking garage, for example, and people have to walk by it to get out of the store or building. In that case, you can opt for a smaller screen if the machine is less expensive. The difference in the price of a larger screen is not always that much, so always go for the bigger screen if you can. If the bigger screen attracts even a few more people per month to use the ATM, it will pay for itself in no time. The only time I don't consider a screen upgrade is in a location I'm unfamiliar with, and more research is needed. For example, is it a good neighborhood? Will the clientele appreciate the big screen, or will it invite vandalism? Is the ATM in clear view from the cash register or other employees? Does the store have security cameras? If so, are they monitored? If the store has bars on the windows, monitored security, or other more aggressive theft prevention measures, I'd feel comfortable about the ATM safety, but I would likely not upgrade the screen.

How to Get Graphics onto Your ATM

The instructions you have to follow for uploading your graphics to the machine differ from model to model. This is why you need to be mindful that your graphics need to be in the proper format and neatly saved into different folders. As far as the process of uploading is concerned, you can do it through a USB stick (flash drive) or an SD card, depending on how your ATM is equipped. Your ATM provider should be able to walk you through this the first time or may offer video tutorials on how this is done correctly to avoid frustration.

Suppose you need help developing the appropriate graphics for your machines. In that case, you can contact a professional to help you. Not only will they design the graphics keeping in mind your brand image, but they will also ensure the files are saved in the proper format. From there on, you only need to upload the files, which can be quickly done by following the instructions. You can create the graphics yourself and load them onto the flash drive, or you can spend about $50 - $100 per screen on graphics if you choose to hire a professional.

Should you choose to process transactions with my firm, we create a welcome screen for you, format it properly based on the ATM purchased, and include it free with every ATM purchase. You can discuss your screen needs with whomever you choose to process or purchase from; hopefully, they will design the appropriate screens for you. They should also save them in the proper format to ensure they run smoothly and you don't face any problems later on.

You can choose any screen size you want. However, the bigger the screen, the easier the machine is to see and use!

PROGRAMMING & INSTALLATION

Programming and installation is one of the critical stages of setting up an ATM business. Your machines must be programmed to be used by customers during the setup. You must ensure they are correctly installed, meaning they are secured to the floor and adhere to ADA requirements. With that in mind, let's examine how this process is completed.

How the ATM is Programmed

Programming involves setting up the machine to be used by customers. Everything from the picture on the screen; when the machine is not in use (the welcome screen) to the denomination of bills to be used in the ATM has to be programmed. In other words, an ATM machine can only be used once it has been correctly programmed. This is why qualified professionals program the machines for you. It's not really that difficult once you know what's needed, but it can be time-consuming if you've never done it before.

Most ATMs are shipped from the factory and must be programmed on-site during installation. ATM manufacturers run a just-in-time (JIT) inventory, and every machine is shipped with their standard operating system (OS). Since the manufacturer doesn't know what ATM processor you plan to use, they ship them in default mode unless your provider offers to preprogram them.

Some ATM providers can have the manufacturer preprogram the ATM for you if you are processing transactions with the same firm you purchase the ATM from. They issue the TID and the master keys, handle all of the configuration settings, and work securely with the manufacturer to set it up correctly. I suggest choosing this option if it's available as it will save you a lot of time. You would still need to change the combination to the safe and change the master password to a 6-digit passcode you can remember when you're logging into the management functions at the ATM as well as uploading the graphics if you want anything custom. Otherwise, the default ATM welcome screen will be shown even if you had the ATM preprogrammed. The default screen is dull.

You can also purchase a standard pre-configured or refurbished machine (when available) if you need it faster. The good news is that these ATM machines can often be programmed before shipping, which means they are ready to use when you receive them. While that is great and saves on installation fees and time, there can be additional fees for shipping or handling of used or reconditioned ATMs. They will still need to be installed at the location, which includes securing them to the floor, connecting power, and establishing communications before use.

Many ATM providers require that professional field technicians complete the ATM programming and master keys if you don't have it preprogrammed. Depending on the location, typical fees can range from $295 –$450, including securing the ATM to the floor and some hands-on training.

If the location is far from a major metropolitan area, there will be fewer technicians. Remote areas can often require techs to drive farther than expected. Emergency and urgent installations can also increase costs. Yes, a professional installation increases your costs the first time. However, unless you are handy and technically inclined, I'd recommend a professional install your first ATM. Then ask your ATM company if you can record the professional installer while installing yours. You can also ask them questions to learn how to do the next one yourself. Most techs will also show you how to operate the ATM if you need that information or want a refresher.

As mentioned earlier, the cheaper option offered by a few companies is to have the manufacturer preprogram the ATM before it ships. Some providers offer a "call-in" or scheduled programming and training by phone, but this is slowly being phased out since now it's the same price as having the manufacturer do it.

Most ISOs and Sub-ISOs will include a programming guide to help you step by step. If you need a lot of help or it's your first time and you want some hand holding, I would suggest finding a coach or an ATM provider that offers some paid training or coaching. You can also check out the YouTube videos my firm offers. Plan on spending an hour or two on the installation. If you want help with programming and get a walk-through of the installation steps at the time of your installation, contact your ATM provider to see if they offer paid phone support or have installation guides and videos.

If your vendor offers some type of paid support, they should take time to answer your questions on the phone or during a coaching session. It will take longer and cost less than a professional coming to your location, but it's about the same price to have it done before your ATM ships. Whether you do the programming or have the manufacturer pre-program it, you would still be responsible for physically installing the ATM, where you bolt the ATM down yourself. You can always hire a professional or even a local handyman if you prefer not to use tools. Drilling into the floor and bolting the ATM down are not difficult but should be done properly to ensure your asset (ATM hardware) and funds are secured. Programming isn't complicated if you can follow the instructions.

Once you install and program a couple of ATMs, you will have the process down. You can do them yourself without assistance or continue using a local handy person. See the resource section for tips on where to get help programming ATMs yourself, as well as programming guides.

However, since programming is critical, if you are not technically savvy, I recommend you go with an experienced professional for your first one and take notes and video so you can opt to do it yourself. Otherwise, have your ATMs preprogrammed if your vendor offers that option.

How the ATM is Installed

There is a proper installation process that needs to be followed:

Before securing the ATM to the floor, be sure to select an area that will meet all of the ADA requirements for space in front of the ATM (enough for wheelchair access). Also, be sure the ATM will be level. Once you secure the ATM to the floor, an uneven surface can warp the sides or leave room for crowbars underneath. The surface on which the machine is to be installed should be flat and level.

The machine has to be securely bolted to the floor. There are pre-drilled holes in the base plate inside the ATM, so all you have to do is drill into the floor. There are two ways you can do this yourself.

First, you can put the ATM in place, then drill the first hole while the ATM is in place. Then, vacuum the hole out and put in the first bolt so the ATM doesn't shift while you drill the second hole in the opposite corner. Then you vacuum and insert the bolt in that hole and do the same to the other two corners to finish bolting the ATM down.

We use a hammer drill. There are many brands and prices. Don't get a cheap one; they won't last. There are many cordless ones as well, but they are much more expensive, and merchants typically have power available. Save your cash and just get one you plug in. If you love cordless tools or you already have several cordless tools, adding a cordless hammer drill is a worthwhile investment.

Drilling with the machine in place can cause extra noise, so if you use this method, you will want to be conscious about who will be around during installation. This is the method of installation that Triton taught 20 years ago. Some people avoid this method because they think there is a risk of getting dust in the dispenser (you can remove it, but it's not necessary) or shaking parts loose. However, I've never had an issue using this method. Keep in mind that if you want to drill the ATM in place, you need a drill that fits under the dispenser. This limits the size of the hammer drill you can buy to be no longer than 12", maybe 13" with the drill bit.

If you're able to do the installation yourself, that's great. An assistant or helper could be programming the ATM while you're bolting it in (or vice versa) if that wasn't completed previously. Sometimes you have to be flexible about the time or the wishes of the store owner depending on the location's floor type. If it's busy when you're completing the installation or if you have someone helping you, be conscious of customers and your surroundings.

The quickest installation method is the one I described. It is much easier to drill and bolt down the machine right the first time with this method since it's almost impossible to drill the holes off-center. Especially if you use ½" bolts instead of ⅜" bolts (the thicker the bolt, the more holding power), you have little margin for error. This way, you also keep the drill holes out of sight from the location owner and staff. Retailers are typically hesitant about drilling holes into the floor to begin with, so drilling them inside the machine is less obvious and prevents having to drill more due to alignment errors.

Another strategy is to mark the holes, move the ATM out of the way, drill all four holes, sweep or vacuum, put the machine back in position, and insert the bolts. This method requires a perfect center punch to ensure exactness in marking holes. While this method is cleaner and potentially safer for the machine, it's easier to make a mistake and can require you to re-drill.

Drilling into tile is a little different, but no big deal as long as you use the right bit. Get a bit for drilling glass (spearhead or diamond core bit) and only use it to go through the tile; otherwise, the concrete may dull the bit unnecessarily. The spear or diamond core will prevent the tile from cracking during drilling. Swap out the bit for the concrete bit once you go through the tile. Don't drill a pilot hole or use a center punch. Instead, put blue tape on the tile, mark it, and start drilling slowly. Don't use hammer mode. The tape should prevent a spear glass bit from wandering. A diamond core bit will cut the full circle and shouldn't wander either way, but the tape can help if the tile is very smooth. A diamond core will make a full-size circle cut, whereas a spear tip will go through the tile easily but will hit the concrete before cutting the tile completely. These diamond core bits are good enough but dull after a few holes. Buy good tools that last if you plan on doing your own installs. Good tools will make the job faster and easier.

You can save time by having one person program the machine while another person drills the holes, but you still have to move the machine back and forth and might need an extension cord. So this method often takes at least 1.5x to 2x longer than the other method and can require a helper.

Regardless of which method is used, you or the installer you hire will want to use a hammer drill with a ½" concrete bit to drill the holes into the floor at least 3.75"- 4" deep. Since concrete slabs are typically 4" thick, it's important not to drill too deep, just deep enough for the bolts. Drilling deeper than 4" may cause you to hit the dirt under the concrete slab. The dirt under the concrete holds moisture, which can eventually erode the bolt, weakening it over time.

You can use special concrete anchors called "redheads" to hammer into the holes. The anchors are what hold the ATM to the floor. I recommend wedge anchors that are ½" x 4.25". Some prefer ⅜" x 3 ¾" stainless steel wedges because they are cheaper. Still, the thicker, longer one is more robust with much higher tension and shear value. (See the resources section for more information.) I also recommend adding some blue tape to a ½" drill bit about 3.5" to 3.75" from the tip. This way, when you drill, you know where to stop so that you leave at least ½" of thread left to add the nut. You can also drill a little more, but no more than just shy of 4".

It's important to note that you must place the redhead through the hole in the base plate of the ATM, then into the concrete. It's also important to note that before hammering the anchor deep into the hole you drilled, place the washer and nut onto the threaded end. If you hammer the threaded end before placing the nut on first, you risk damaging the threads, making it difficult, if not impossible, to put the nut on after.

Plug the ATM into a power outlet only after the ATM is appropriately secured to the floor. A 110V/AC outlet is required for this purpose. I recommend a dedicated circuit. If a dedicated outlet is unavailable, be sure to use a surge protector, and if you're concerned about power outages, get one with a battery backup with at least a 1000-joule rating. I recommend any of these over 650VA.

Lastly, the machine has to be connected to communicate with the ATM processor via the merchant's internet connection or a wireless communication device. As I previously mentioned, the best approach is to use a separate dedicated wireless device or the location's high-speed internet connection if it's reliable. I prefer to use a wireless device so I'm in control of my own communication device.

The average ATM machine weighs between 160 and 250 pounds. So, the machine isn't heavier than a large safe. This is why it's important to secure it to the floor properly.

You can install it on your own, hire a professional ATM technician to do the job for you, or work with your ATM provider to coordinate the installation. No matter which option you choose, make sure the installation is done thoroughly and properly.

> It's important to note that you must place the redhead through the hole in the base plate of the ATM, then into the concrete and place the washer and nut onto the threaded end first. If you hammer the threaded end before placing the nut on first, you risk damaging the threads, making it difficult, if not impossible, to put the nut on after.

CASH

Most privately owned ATMs are just vending machines that dispense $20 instead of products. Customers can only perform a few functions through these ATMs, which include cash transactions, balance inquiries, and transfers.

Several ATM manufacturers, specifically Hyosung, have added functions like MoneyGram and Bill Pay to their software. The networks have been working to certify additional equipment and functionality, such as a bill acceptor in an ATM sidecar or an ATM Kiosk, for these functions. If you're just starting in the ATM business, be sure your selected vendor is aware of this and can offer you this functionality if you want it.

How Much Cash the Machine Holds

The amount of cash your machine will hold depends on the cassette you select. Cassettes vary in size from 700, 1,000, or 2,000 notes. There are fixed cassettes, which are being phased out, and two types of removable cassettes. Fixed note cassettes hold 700 notes. Removable cassette options hold 1,000 or 2,000 notes. Of course, that is the maximum number of bills you can load. I recommend starting with $2,000 - $3,000 (100-150 used notes) and monitoring your ATM usage so that you can best determine the right amount of cash needed. Once you have a better idea of the number of transactions performed on your machine, you can maximize your cash loading. Remember that paydays, holiday weekends, and certain times of the year are busier than others, depending on the location. It's best to monitor this closely and set low balance alerts so you don't run out of cash.

How Frequently to Put Cash in the Machine

As the owner of the business, it is up to you to decide the time at which you would reload the machine. However, rather than complicate this, you can simply log into your online ATM dashboard, review your ATM balance, or set up text/SMS alerts.

Online monitoring is typically done through your service company portal. Ensure that the company you process with offers an online portal. You'll need this to help manage your ATM business, and it's much easier if you're able to log in to view your ATMs remotely from anywhere.

Once you become an IAD and get your paperwork done and get your first ATM installed, your business name and email address will be used to create an online profile for your ATMs so you can log in and review all the info, set up alerts, and view all the transactions in real time.

When your ATM begins to get low on cash, you should plan to load it as soon as possible. You can also set up a schedule once you know the busy days. For example, suppose the ATM is busy on weekends. In that case, you should ensure sufficient funds are available in the ATM before Friday rolls around.

Again, the volume of transactions your machine attracts will play a major role in determining how frequently you need to put cash into it. It is possible that you won't put more than fifty $20 bills in the machine at first. It might suffice, but the situation will change if the number of customers increases. In that case, you will have to load more cash or increase the frequency of putting money into the machine.

Maximum Surcharge

Most states in the U.S. don't have any legal limit for the surcharge fee you can impose on each transaction performed on your machine. There have been cities and states that propose setting limits, but none have passed as of this writing.

However, that doesn't mean you can charge any amount you wish. For instance, if the average withdrawal transaction is $60, you would not want to charge $10. That would mean the customer must spend a substantial percentage of the withdrawn amount for the withdrawal. There is a point of diminishing returns.

If the surcharge fee is too high, it can actually drive people away from your machine. This is why the surcharge fee you set for your machines must be competitive but not too low. Check the resource section for a link to see the highest ATM fees in various cities.

While the maximum surcharge does not depend on any legal limit, some states have restrictions. Rather than list all of the states here, you have to research the surcharge fees being charged in your vicinity and then decide your rate accordingly. Also, you need to keep in mind the location of your ATM. For instance, ATMs located in retail stores cannot charge a surcharge fee as high as those in a casino or other typical higher surcharge venues.

Here are some guidelines for how you can set the surcharge:

- $1.50 to $3.50 – fast food restaurants, nail salons, barbershops, tattoo shops

- $2.95 to $4.95 – nightclubs, bars and grills, convenience stores, temporary Halloween stores, Christmas tree lots, events, and most other locations
- $5.00 and over – casinos, adult entertainment establishments, and parking lots
- ATMs with high withdrawal amounts can have a flat rate or a percent, whichever is greater—often 1% to 1.5%. We have one set at $4 or 2%, but that is in a downtown parking lot with many tourists across the street from a popular concert venue.

These are just general numbers based on observations of what ATMs in these types of businesses usually charge their customers. Based on my experience, the ideal range for setting a surcharge fee to get the customers accustomed to using your ATM and getting it to "ramp up" is $1.95 to $2.95. I know several machines charging just $1.00, some charging $3.95 or more, and some with no surcharge. It all depends on the location. In this regard, I recommend you speak with your ATM provider to determine the maximum surcharge for a new location, not just the best surcharge. Personally, I think it's best to start a little lower than ATMs in the surrounding area and then slowly increase it once the machine gets busy. No one will notice a $0.25 - $0.50 surcharge increase unless it crosses a psychological threshold—$ 2.95 to $3.25 or $3.50 to $4.00, for example. Going from $2.50 to $2.95 or $3.25 to $3.50 rarely changes the usage. I don't recommend using odd surcharges, which can make it memorable; stick with increments of 5. You don't want customers thinking that the ATM charges $3.49 or $3.69.... Stick to the norms of what other ATMs are charging in your area already.

How Passive Income is Paid

ATM providers have different dates when they pay the residual commissions. This is the surcharge and any interchange portion of your revenue and is separate from your settlement funds (the money you load the ATM with). Some ATM providers will pay the surcharge daily.

Pros of daily surcharge:

1. It gets your cash flow started if you're tight when starting.

Cons of daily surcharge:

1. Creates an accounting headache.
2. It more than doubles the number of deposits to your bank account.
3. Tracking becomes more difficult.
4. It can cause extra bank charges.

I prefer an ATM provider to send residual commissions once a month. If you know your ATM provider has been in business for decades and is servicing thousands of ATMs, they ensure you get paid. My firm offers both options and pays anyone else you instruct us to pay (as indicated on the ACH forms).

Most ATM providers send commissions between the 7th and 10th of each month following the month the transactions take place. Some send a few days later. If your ATM vendor doesn't send commissions by the 15th of the month, they use your cash flow or may have cash flow problems, so that's a warning.

For example, if you tell your ATM provider on your documents package that your ATM will surcharge $3.00 and you want them to pay your location $1.00 after the first fifty transactions, they should be able to do that. So starting on the 51st transaction each month, the location owner would get $1.00 from every fee charged.

Want to pay your Uncle Joe $0.25 per transaction for helping you? Make sure your ATM vendor can do that as well. Want to pay several different people? Make sure the ATM vendor you select offers this. If you let them know whom to pay and how much, they should take care of that so you can concentrate on your business. If they don't offer this service, you must do the accounting, make the payments, and send the year-end 1099s yourself.

Just make sure you understand what, if any, fees they charge for this service. They will be responsible for sending the funds. They should also mail 1099s at the end of the year to you and anyone you have them pay. That's a big accounting headache they will take care of for you. After paying everyone you tell your ATM provider to pay, your account will be credited with the remaining residual commissions, less any network fees.

LOADING AND RELOADING THE ATM

How Much Cash to Load

The amount of cash you need to load into the machine depends on a few factors.

The first factor is the cassette type. The type of cassette installed will determine the maximum cash limits; however, it is rarely, if ever, necessary to fill the machines to capacity. There are two types of cassettes, and some machines can handle multiple cassettes for extremely busy locations. Still, most machines you see in retail stores are single-cassette ATMs.

Fixed note cassettes typically hold 700-1,000 notes (closer to 700 recycled versus new bills). Removable cassettes typically hold 1,000-2,000 notes, which, again, is more than enough for most locations.

Second, you don't want to use brand-new notes in your ATM, as they tend to stick together and are unsuitable for ATM use. Your bank should give you "ATM currency" (recycled currency) in banded packets of $1,000 if you get ten-dollar bills or $2,000 if you get twenty-dollar bills. A typical fixed cassette will hold approximately $14,000 in twenties, which should be more than enough cash if you load your ATM weekly. If it's using more than this due to a high withdrawal average, think about adding a percentage surcharge so you make more money. Do this when you don't mind loading more often or need to upgrade to a bigger-cassette machine.

The third factor is how busy the location is. You can determine your maximum cash requirements by estimating how many transactions you will get daily. Let's say you think the ATM would produce five transactions daily. If the average withdrawal is $80, the machine will need at least $400 per day. How often you want to load it will determine how much you need to load at a time. Suppose you want to visit the machine every ten days, using this example. In that case, I suggest you load at least $3,500 - $4,000 and then monitor it using real-time online monitoring (your ATM company should provide this).

You can check the online monitoring system as often as you like to see the cash run rate and real-time transactions so you can adjust the cash amounts until you get the timing down. Still, it's easy to use the ATM alert system and get text messages on your phone when the ATM is running low. You don't want to set the alerts for too low a balance; otherwise, it can run out, especially if you need additional time to pick up the cash and drive to the location. I suggest setting the low balance alert for at least two days of your current run rate as the low balance alert. That gives you enough time to get cash in an emergency.

An emergency would be an unexpected day to need to load cash. Suppose you load your ATMs on Thursdays to ensure plenty of cash for weekends. Now, suppose your bank gets their armored delivery on Wednesdays. You want to call in your vault cash order (if it's not a standing order) late Monday or early Tuesday so they can order it with their normal armored delivery on Wednesday. You want to pick it up within 24 hours of the delivery since the bank ordered it for you and they can get charged for it if it's not withdrawn. You don't want to cause your bank unnecessary expenses.

Suppose your ATM had a great Friday and Saturday night, and you get a text alert on Sunday afternoon. Or suppose your average withdrawal over the weekend was an anomaly (maybe there was some event you weren't aware of—it happens). In that case, you must load more cash before the next armored delivery, but the bank is closed.

You can always pull $1,000 from your bank's ATM to put into your ATM in an emergency; however, if it's really busy, $1,000 might not be enough. Therefore, I recommend keeping an extra couple grand in $20s handy for emergencies. If you get a low cash alert, you can grab your emergency cash and/or go to your bank ATM to pull out the max your bank will allow.

Pro Tip: Ask your banker about increasing the default ATM withdrawal maximum for your vault cash account and keep the ATM card handy for emergencies.

Suppose you know about an event, high-usage weekend, or holiday when banks are closed. In that case, you can load as much extra cash as possible in anticipation of the usage.

You can start with a $500 alert depending on the usage, but play it safe and make the best use of your cash flow so your ATMs don't run out. You also do not want to leave too much in there between planned loads, so try to estimate 2 days' worth for an alert.

Depending on how busy the location can be, I recommend loading at least $2,000 to start. If you don't have that much cash initially, you can start with less, even as little as $500. But remember, if your machine runs out of money, you're out of business.

The funds are deposited into your account the next business day, so you can withdraw them and put them back into the machine. However, you don't want to run out of cash on weekends when banks will not be open. As mentioned, you can use your bank's ATM in an emergency to get more money for your ATM on weekends. Also, remember that since banks are not open on weekends or holidays, money doesn't move through the banking system, so the cash dispensed from your ATM Friday through Sunday is deposited back into your account the following Monday. Remember that bank holidays that fall on a Friday or Monday don't process transactions until the next business day.

If you need help determining the amount of cash for a specific location, your ATM company should be able to help you to determine what's best.

Who Loads the ATM

As the machine owner, you can load the ATM yourself, have the store owner load cash, hire a vaulting service, or even pay for armored car services.

Loading the cash yourself is the most profitable way to operate your ATM business. It is a simple process, as you can see from this how to load cash video on YouTube. While this video (linked in the resources section) shows an older-style cassette and dispenser, it's similar to most models, except for the dispenser rotation, which many older Triton ATMs still use, so I no longer recommend those dispensers. The turning mechanism has been known to become an issue over time. This is a video of loading cash in a new Hyosung ATM.

If you have less than a couple dozen ATMs, you can create a weekly, bi-weekly, or three-times-per-month schedule to load cash. We recommend alternating load days and times so you don't fall into a pattern someone could notice and predict. I also know some ATM operators who hire off-duty police or plain clothes security to accompany them a few times a month if they are venturing into neighborhoods where they are uncomfortable. Suppose you're a frequent customer of the establishment where you have the ATM installed (which is how many ATM owners start out). In that case, it's perfectly normal for you to visit the location often. You can even make arrangements with store owners or building managers to load the ATM during closed or off-hours, and many store owners let ATM operators load cash in their back office. This is where a removable cassette comes in handy.

If you vault your ATM machine with your own cash, there are some steps you need to follow to balance the funds in your bank account to confirm your total cash value. First, add up the funds inside the ATM cassette (or a trial cassette total from the management functions will give you that amount). Next, add the current funds amount inside your bank account. Last, add up the withdrawal transaction amounts (from the online portal under real-time transactions) for all withdrawal transactions that occurred after 3pm EST the previous day through your current time of day. The total number will confirm the total cash value for your designated bank account. I've included a document with the entire step by step process in the resource section.

You can delegate the cash-loading service if you have a business partner or trusted employees. You can also wait until the machines start running low on cash (using SMS alerts) and just load them whenever you need to instead of having a specific schedule. This method requires you to keep some money somewhere accessible besides the bank account in case you need to load on a weekend or holiday. If you use the 2-day rule for alerts, you might still have time to get to the bank, but it will be challenging to schedule your pickups, so it's best to keep a schedule with your bank however you decide to load.

Another popular method to load cash is to have the store owner do it daily. Typically, store owners would load about $500 - $1,000 before opening each day and remove any remaining funds when closing. They balance the ATM just like a cash register, except the ATM is only one denomination, so it's much more manageable. The only issue is when the store owner forgets, gets lazy, has a sick day, or doesn't have enough cash flow that day to load cash. In those cases, you are basically out of business until the store owner loads the ATM again. You may also have to share more of the surcharge income with the store owner to load cash, reducing your profits.

You can also hire a third party vaulting service or pay for armored car services. These options can be paid using the surcharge proceeds on a per-transaction basis through some vendors. If your vendor quotes a flat rate, it might be costly, so make sure you have a busy ATM or want to outsource this function before committing to these options. However, these options open up many more possibilities for placing ATMs farther from your home.

Most ATM operators start by loading the ATM themselves, and if the ATM is very busy or has too many ATMs to load, then contracting out the vaulting is a way to grow the business. Vaulting fees range from $1.50 down to $0.60 per withdrawal transaction, depending on transaction volume and cash requirements. Armored services can be per transaction or flat rates between $180 and $225 per drop. It really depends on how busy the ATM is, how much cash is needed, and how often it needs to be filled.

Essentially, you, the owner, decide when you want the cash loaded and who will do it.

Fixed Note Cassettes

There are two types of ATM cassettes. First is the fixed note cassette. This cassette type is fixed into the machine and cannot be removed. You have to load the cash into the machine where it is bolted in (similar to a napkin holder where you slide back a pressure plate and insert the cash). However, fixed note cassettes are being phased out. Only the Genmega GT3000 TTW model is still manufactured with this option as of this printing. If you're considering used or refurbished ATMs, check the cassette type.

There are some pros and cons of fixed note cassettes.

Pros

- ATMs with fixed note cassettes are cheaper than those with removable cassettes.
- The capacity of a typical fixed note cassette is sufficient (700-1,000 notes, depending on the manufacturer) for a busy location.
- You don't have to remove any components or parts from the ATM to reload the cash. Simply open up the cassette and insert the money.
- They load quickly: insert key, lift up door, insert cash, lock cassette.

Cons

- You must load the cash where the ATM is (usually in a busy area). You cannot remove the cassette and take it to a secure location where you would feel safe loading the cash.
- You can't have an "extra" cassette pre-loaded to swap out.
- There is typically a smaller capacity for both cassette and reject tray. If the cassette is fixed, the reject tray is also not removable.

Typical Fixed Note Cassette Specs:

> Cash Dispenser (CDU) Type: Drawer type (fixed)
> Maintenance: Front Service Type
> Cassette Capacity: 700-1,000 Notes
> Reject Capacity: Reject Box: 100 Notes
> Dispense Speed: 2 Notes/sec

Note Pick Up: Friction

Power Supply: DC24V, 5V

Dimension: 250mm*220mm*360mm(W*H*D)

Weight: < 7kg

Removable Cassettes

Removable cassettes can be taken out of or removed from the machine to be reloaded. There are pros and cons of removable cassettes as well.

Pros

- The most obvious pro is that you can remove the cassette from the ATM and take it to a safe and discreet location for loading the cash. This gives you greater security when dealing with a large amount of money.
- Removable cassettes offer you the ability to have a spare cassette. This means you can load it faster. You load a spare cassette at home or in your office and simply swap them at the location to load the cash. Whenever the cassette in the machine starts to run low on money, load the other one and simply replace the empty cassette with it.
- They are considered an upgrade or are typically part of higher-end ATMs.
- Removable cassettes also come in a multi-cassette dispenser configuration with two different denominations. This provides twice as much cash for busy locations or places where loading $10s and $20s or different denominations would increase profits.
- They provide near-end detection and note shortage detection, which can help to reduce reversals or journal requests.

Cons

- When you frequently remove and install the cassette, there is more wear and tear, so just be cautious when handling it often.
- Removable cassettes are generally considered an upgrade that increases the price of the ATM, but most ATMs come with them now.

Typical Removable Cassette Specs:

> CDU Type: Cassette (removable)
>
> Maintenance: Front Service
>
> Cassette Capacity: Max. 1,000, 1,700, and 2,000 notes depending on the model (rated for new US notes); typically hold less for recycled currency
>
> Reject Capacity: Reject Bin: Max. 200 notes
>
> Dispense Speed: 3 Sheets/sec
>
> Note Pick Up: Friction
>
> Power Supply: DC24V, 5V
>
> Dimension: 270mm*295mm*430mm(W*H*D)
>
> Weight: < 10kg
>
> Near-End Detection: Yes
>
> Note Shortage Detection: Yes

Which Cassette to Use

Since fixed note cassettes can really only be found in a new Genmega GT3000 or used and refurbished machines, there isn't much of a choice regarding the cassette type for free-standing ATMs. Your decision comes down to how busy the location will be and whether you need a 1,000-note cassette, a 2,000-note cassette, or two 1,000-note cassettes. Often referred to as 1K and 2K cassettes, they hold closer to 800-1,700 recycled notes, which is plenty for most locations.

If you think the location is going to be busy, I personally recommend getting two 1,000-note cassettes instead of opting for one larger 2,000-note cassette. Here's why:

First, a single 2K cassette or two 1K cassettes cost the same to upgrade. As of this publication, each option is about $400.

Second, two cassettes gives you more options. You can load two different denominations or double the normal denomination at a busy location. The ATM can still run on one cassette if you need the other cassette for another ATM or if one cassette has an issue or needs to be sent in for repairs without leaving you out of business. It's a cheap way to keep one cassette as a spare, maybe for a machine that can handle high traffic, seasonal highs, or a high withdrawal average. Two cassettes is a great option for busy locations where you charge a percentage due to high withdrawal amounts.

Removable cassettes used to be considered an upgrade, but ATM manufacturers saw the value in making most new ATMs come standard with removable cassettes and eLocks to make it easier for everyone. That did increase the price of the ATM a little but not as much as when they were optional. Since all ATMs come that way, now everyone benefits from the economy of scale.

Best Denominations to Use

An important consideration that only a few ATM business owners pay attention to is the denominations of bills they use. You can go as low as $1 and as high as $100. Which are the best denominations to use for ATMs?

At this time, nearly every ATM in the United States dispenses only $20 bills. Before that, banks also dispensed $5 and $10, but $20 became standard. This is because sticking to one denomination is cheaper and more efficient, and the $20 is the most prevalent denomination. There are different bins, or cassettes, for each denomination, each with a specific capacity. You must install a dispenser with multiple cassettes to use other denominations.

Therefore, it is much more convenient to stick to $20s. Twenty-dollar bills provide a balance between the highest and lowest possible withdrawals. That being said, serving odd numbers like $55 becomes difficult. However, most ATM users are accustomed to using the quick cash withdrawal features anyway.

When you initially set up your ATM and submit your paperwork, you must tell the ATM service provider what denomination you will be loading. However, suppose you accidentally load $10s into a machine that thinks it's dispensing $20s. In that case, your customers will be shorted, and you will get complaint notices and automated reversals. Also, if you load $20s into a machine set up to dispense $10s, you'll give customers twice as much. And you won't have a way to recover these funds unless you get an honest ATM user to call you. This is why I recommend completing a transaction yourself and taking out at least the minimum amount every time you load the ATM. Completing a withdrawal on your own ATM will let you know whether it's working correctly, help to prevent any mistakes, and avoid trips back to the location due to a jam or improper load (rare but it can happen). I have learned this from experience. Pay yourself the surcharge and conduct a withdrawal. It will save you in the long run. If your bank charges a foreign ATM fee, sign up for an internet bank that does not charge, or work with an institution that will reimburse you for a specific number of them monthly.

There is no clear answer to what denomination is the most profitable. It typically depends on the needs of the people who frequent the area where your ATM is located. While banks prefer you load $20s, as they are the most common denomination and obtainable from the bank, loading some machines with $10s can be more profitable. And in some cases, loading $5s can be terrific. If you have an ATM located near vending machines, a self-service car wash, or a laundromat, many of the bill acceptors, unless it's a new or recently remodeled facility, only accept $5s or $10s. So be sure to check this if you plan to operate an ATM in these venues.

I've also seen that dispensing $10 bills in ATMs in less desirable neighborhoods with off-brand liquor and convenience stores, for example, or stores in less affluent neighborhood areas or where many businesses and homes might have bars on windows and doors, do better dispensing $10s. Individuals receiving government benefits or living in low-income areas may not have significant balances in their accounts. These individuals often appreciate increments of $10 since their average withdrawal amount is usually less than the national mean.

THE PROCESS

It's time to learn how withdrawals are made and how you get your money back. You must understand the process thoroughly, so this is an important chapter.

Getting Money Back into Your Account

The cash in the machine comes from the cash vaulter's account. If you own the ATM machine, you must decide who will load the cash. This person is the vaulter. If you decide to put your money into the machine, you would be the ATM owner, operator, and vaulter, which is how to make the most money.

As the owner, you are responsible for ensuring the machine does not run out of cash. If you have delegated the vaulting duties to a third party or vaulting service provider, those responsibilities will transfer to them. Most ATM companies offer some type of vaulting service.

After a few months, you will have a clear idea of the peak hours and prime days during which withdrawals will be busier than usual. Suppose you are doing the cash loading yourself. In that case, you can use your ATM vendor's online system to keep track of the cash balance in the ATM to help you manage the replenishment cycle so the machine does not run out of cash. You can also ensure you are not loading more money than necessary.

So, if you put your cash into the machine and people withdraw it, how do you get it back? The ATM company you work with or their third-party provider will move the money into your account via Automated Clearing House (ACH) via the Federal Reserve Banking System. You will receive a deposit for each day's ATM transactions on the following business banking day.

The cut-off time for my ATMs is from 1:00 pm to 12:59 pm PT. For example, suppose someone uses my ATMs here in California between Monday at 1:00 pm and Tuesday at 12:59 pm. In that case, all the funds withdrawn between those times are returned to my bank account on Wednesday morning. The ACH happens the previous day overnight, so your bank credits your account the next morning. In the example above, the funds move through the Federal Reserve on Tuesday evening. They are credited to my settlement account Wednesday morning.

Since the weekends and holidays are not banking days, funds withdrawn between Friday at 1:00 pm and Sunday at 12:59 pm are deposited on Monday as three separate deposits, one for each day. If Friday or Monday happens to be a holiday, the deposit gets pushed back to Tuesday.

Make sure you ask the ATM company you work with to tell you their daily cash settlement policy so that you know the exact schedule for funds returning to your account.

Cash settlement timing varies among ATM providers. Ensure you understand the schedule, which can significantly affect your business's cash flow. A good service deposits money into your account on Tuesday for withdrawals made on Monday, like in the example above. So, if you are in New York and work with an ATM provider on the west coast, all funds withdrawn before 4:00 pm ET on Monday would be deposited back into the settlement account on Tuesday.

Some ATM providers delay settlement to use the float since most are moving millions of dollars, and one extra day delay can make a big difference to them and you. If you have a lot of ATMs and you are the vaulter, you want the fastest settlement possible.

Some vaulters arrange for bank cash. They work with the local banker who wants to put the bank's money to work. Yes, some banks do this. It's not something they advertise. Suppose you want to offer a vaulting program for your ATM business. In that case, you can create a business plan and pitch it to as many local bankers as possible. Financial institutions understand the ATM business. Developing the right banking relationships to become a vaulter using the bank's money takes a while. It's FDIC insured, so you need to get bonded and would need specialty insurance, but it's all possible in the world of the ATM business. A large vaulter might have half a million or more of the bank's money at work. It's all about the percentage they can make and understanding and agreeing to the process.

The Withdrawal Process

If you've ever used an ATM, you know how this works. Skip to the next page. If not, an ATM is a convenient way to withdraw cash from a bank account. This is why people prefer using machines instead of going to the bank. The process for withdrawal is quite simple, which makes ATMs so popular. The customer simply has to insert his or her debit or credit card (depending on the machine) into the dip or swipe reader on the machine.

The machine then prompts the customer to enter his or her PIN, and the instructions for withdrawing are displayed on the screen. The customer doesn't have to think about what to do. The process is the same for practically all ATMs to make it even easier.

WORKING WITH YOUR BANK

Choosing the Right Bank

There are lots of banks out there to choose from, and the right banking relationship can save you time and money. I recommend starting with a bank you already have a relationship with.

The easiest way to manage your ATM deposits is by opening a separate bank account for your ATM business unless you already have a business account with a bank. The processor will automatically make deposits into your bank account every business day for vault cash. At the same time, there shouldn't be a lot of transactions going through your account— thirty or so deposits monthly (three deposits on Monday, then one deposit each other business day).

Managing ATM vault cash is time-consuming when the deposits are combined with your regular business transactions in the same account. I suggest a separate checking account for your ATM vault cash to make it easier. This can help you track the money you allocate for loading ATMs. You can always start with one account, and if you discover that you don't like all of your funds for all of your ATMs in the same account, open a separate account. Be sure to complete a new ACH for your ATM provider whenever you make bank account changes. You only have to complete one form but know it may take a few days to reflect the changes to the settlement funds account.

Ask your banker about fees for deposits and what the limits are. For example, if the account includes up to 200 transactions (they usually mean ACH deposits) monthly, you can calculate how many ATMs you can use that account for before additional fees might be levied. There should be fewer than thirty total deposits for each ATM each month. Banks can have different fee structures for different checking account types. A basic checking account with a low daily balance may have a monthly fee. You must compare accounts and fees that best suit your business model and immediate goals. You can always upgrade or downgrade the account.

Each time your ATM is low on cash, you must visit the bank and withdraw the funds from your account to reload the ATM. This could bring your account to a zero balance if you use all available funds to reload cash. When opening a new account with the bank, ask about an account with no monthly fees (or at least the lowest possible fees; many banks offer accounts that cost less than $10.00 per month). It's also a good idea to mention that the balance could reach zero dollars for a day or two a month.

Remember that all banks operate differently and have different criteria for maintaining accounts. For example, your bank may impose a daily minimum balance requirement of $100.00 or more. Therefore, you must maintain a daily balance of $100.00 to avoid the monthly fees. The simple solution would always be to keep an extra $100.00 in your account to avoid any fees, but sometimes that's impossible. So, if you have $1,000.00 in your account for reloading cash and you need it all, leave at least $20 since you will most likely receive a deposit the next day if your ATM is busy enough. Talk to the banker to get the best account for your needs. It's an average daily balance for the entire month. For example, if you had at least $200 in the account for two weeks of the month, $20 in it for a week, and then various other amounts the rest of the month over $20, the account would still have an average daily balance of over $100.

Other banks may ask you to set up a savings account to link to your business account with an automatic monthly transfer of $100.00 from checking to savings. This is another easy way to avoid paying fees. You can quickly transfer the money back to your checking account a few days after the automatic transfer. You can also set up overdraft protection, but find out what the associated fees would be.

Whatever bank you select, just make sure you account for any fees and keep a ledger so you always balance your cash monthly. Your vault cash will either be in the bank account, the ATM, or in transit on the way to your bank.

Cash Needs

Introducing yourself to the merchant teller and your bank's branch manager is a good idea. You want to ensure they know your business and cash needs if you didn't meet them when setting up your account.

Everyone wants to know how much they should load the first time. A good starting amount is $2,000-$3,000 each week per machine.

The merchant teller usually orders cash for the branch and will want to ensure they can accommodate your needs. Banks typically have several thousand in $20s available but may need to special-order $10s in case you need them. Discuss your cash needs with them when you open the account so you know the process before you install your first ATM. If you add more machines later, you'll need to inform the bank, add it to your ATM audit for the future, and increase your cash order as needed.

Adhering to the following suggestions can make you more attractive to work with, make the process more efficient, and save you money in fees:

- Pick up your cash on a set day every week. Sometimes, the armored carriers that bring money to the banks make deposits on a specific day of the week. If you can pick it up on that same day, the bank will pay less interest.
- Call ahead. Give the merchant teller ample time to have your cash ready. This will save you time waiting at the branch and help keep the lines moving.
- Write a withdrawal slip. Fill it out in advance for each account. Be sure to include all of your account information and cash totals.
- Be prepared and professional.
- Show appreciation for the job they do for you. Bringing the merchant teller a gift during the holidays and his or her birthday goes a long way in building a relationship.

Cash loading is simple if you are just starting off and loading $20s into only one ATM. You can even pull all of your cash-loading funds directly from the ATM at your bank. As previously mentioned, most banks will allow you to increase the maximum withdrawal amount on your debit card to at least $600. Depending on their policy, some banks will increase it to $1,000 or even more. The higher limit allows you to withdraw money from the bank's ATM if necessary.

You might need special permission from the bank to have a higher-than-standard limit. Still, considering your line of business, it should be approved. This will help you save time and access cash even when the banks are closed on Sundays. Remember that having a high withdrawal limit is a convenience and security risk. If your bank card and PIN are stolen, the thief can access more of your account. This is rare, but it's good to know anyway.

Cash Loading Safety Tips:

- Try to load cash on alternating days and times, different from an exact schedule every week or month.
- Try to load cash during daylight hours.
- Keep cash in your pocket or an unmarked bag.
- Try to maintain a low profile.
- Have someone accompany you the first few times.
- When opening the safe with the combination, try to cover the numbers with your free hand, and always assume you are being watched.

OWNERSHIP & RESPONSIBILITIES

Owning an ATM brings with it a set of responsibilities. You will be responsible for ensuring that the machine remains up and running throughout the day and that there is minimal downtime—the machine must be working for you to make money. You need to take care of the legalities of running an ATM business and bear the costs of keeping the ATM operational.

This means that there are several things to take care of. As the owner, you have to be in charge. It is better to keep things under control and ensure everything goes smoothly. Of course, you can delegate the responsibilities to people you trust. Next, let's distinguish who owns the ATM.

Who Owns the ATM

You might need clarification on this title. After all, since you ordered the ATM, you own it, right? Undoubtedly, the person who orders the ATM, pays for it, and has it installed is the one who owns it. But, at the same time, you have to consider that the location where you are installing the machine might be owned by someone else.

If you found an empty storefront, retail space, kiosk, or another type of space and rented it, you retained ownership of the machine. However, when you use the space in someone else's store or business, you will likely have to share some revenue with them. So, does the other party own the ATM if it's installed on their premises?

The short answer is no. In this case, you become their ATM placement provider. The agreement between you and the location is called a site location agreement (SLA). You agree to place an ATM on their site, and they are agreeing to let you use that space and to provide electricity. The SLA will clearly name the business where you are installing the ATM as the location and your name as the owner.

Of course, the terms and conditions you write with the other party may vary, but that doesn't mean you cede ownership. So, even if you have to share revenue with the location, you remain the ATM owner and reap the benefits of the fixed asset and its depreciation for tax purposes.

Who Loads the ATM

Well, this is the million-dollar question (or the thousand-dollar one, at least). The person who loads the ATM is known as the ATM vaulter. The biggest responsibility you must bear when operating an ATM business is determining who is loading the ATM. Most ATM business owners load their own machines until they start growing the business. Loading the cash a few times a month is not a big ordeal.

It will take a while for you to determine how often to load it and how much cash each machine will need to be efficient. You can project the number of transactions you expect on the machine from the outset. However, whether that number is accurate can only be determined over time.

On average, an on-site ATM machine owner may load forty to fifty $20 bills into the ATM machine daily or every other day. However, you would likely be an off-site owner since you will not be at the location daily. You should load enough money so the ATM does not run out for at least a week once you know the pattern. You don't want to load the ATM every other day. The number of transactions on your machine may exceed your expectations, so you'll need to put in a hundred or so 20s (which would be great). Just plan accordingly.

Regardless of the number of transactions, it is a good idea to check up on your machine at least once a day or every other day, even if you don't need to load it. This can be done remotely via the Internet if you're working with an ATM provider that offers an online real-time portal.

If you are on-site, meaning you work in the store or very close by, and you don't have much cash to load, you might need to load the machine daily. This is why it is essential to determine who will load the machine. In most cases, the owner chooses to do this on his or her own.

However, you can also get someone to do the job for you. Ensure the person you select is trustworthy, appropriately trained, and knows how to operate the machine and load the cassette. If you don't feel you have someone worthy of the task, it is better to do it yourself or to talk to your ATM company and ask if they offer cash vaulting.

If you manage your own vaulting, at least you can rest assured that the machine is always full of cash, and there is no risk of you being swindled. Remember that if you're loading the ATM, it is most likely your money unless you use the OPM method. When you arrange to work with private investors like friends and family, take on a business partner with access to cash, or work with a financial institution, that is other people's money. Just don't exaggerate returns, and be transparent about the business. You'll find people like the investment possibilities.

When installing a machine in someone else's store, you can ask the store owner to be the vaulter as part of the arrangement. Even though the store owner will only be the location owner and not the ATM owner, this does not mean he or she cannot be responsible for loading the ATM. Both parties can benefit if you cannot or prefer not to load cash. Or, if the security isn't up to your requirements for your "free placement program," you can tell them they don't qualify for a full placement with vaulting. Still, if they would like to load cash, you can install the ATM. Then negotiate the surcharge share to see if it makes business sense.

There are pros and cons to having the store owner be the vaulter. These are some pros:

- Several fewer responsibilities for you as the owner.
  - o No trip to the bank for that ATM
  - o Fewer trips to the location
  - o No balancing or cash to account for
- You also can use your money to purchase more equipment.
- The store can load much less daily and empty the ATM each evening.

The pro for the store owner is that it ensures the machine won't run out of cash; however, if they forget to load the money, have a health issue and didn't delegate the responsibility, or cash is not always available, your machine will run out of money anyway, which is a con for you. You would also expect to give the store owner more of the surcharge share to use his or her cash to load the ATM.

I suggest you load cash for your first few machines to experience the entire business process. Suppose you are unable to load some money. In that case, your ATM provider may be able to provide you with a vaulter, but expect to pay either a flat fee or a flat per transaction charge for this service. It's best to place your first few machines within a ten to twenty-mile radius of your home or office so that you can service them properly and get to know the business. Once you've got some experience under your belt, you'll find many other natural opportunities within the business.

The bottom line is that it isn't necessarily the same person who owns and loads the ATM. It is a responsibility that can be delegated to someone else. You have to decide what's convenient for you in the long run. If you plan to set up a dozen ATMs all over town or in a nearby city, you may need some assistance getting the machines loaded.

The ownership and responsibilities related to the ATM machine should be decided upon before the site location agreement is drawn up. Some locations prefer to own the ATM and have someone else load and service it or just buy it and load it themselves and have you service it.

ATM Management vs. ATM Placement

You can outsource the entire process and management of installing, maintaining, and operating the ATM you have purchased to an ATM management company. This kind of agreement is known as ATM management. Rather than operating the ATM on your own, you hire an ATM management company to do it for you. The company you select will charge fees for each service you wish to have managed. If you purchase the ATM, you can have the management company load cash and handle maintenance and all of the other functions or just some of them. It's up to you which parts you wish to have managed.

What you get in return with complete ATM management is absolute comfort. You can rest assured that all things related to the installation and operation of your machines are under control. You only have to inform the company where you want the ATM installed; they will do everything for you.

The services offered will vary from company to company. If you prefer this arrangement, select an ATM vendor for this purpose. Ensure they offer this and have followed through on those promises by checking reviews and speaking with people. The fees for this service can outweigh the profits. You need high transaction processing locations, at least 250-300 monthly surcharged transactions at $2.50 or more for this business model to work. Discuss your needs with your ATM provider.

An ATM placement is an arrangement where an ATM company or IAD places an ATM in a location and owns and operates all aspects of the ATM machine. The location owner would receive a small percentage of the revenue generated from the ATM in return for letting the IAD place the ATM at the location. If you are considering investing in ATMs as a business, you would be the IAD, and you would typically want to find locations that want placements. You would then work with your ATM provider to help you operate your ATMs profitably and select the right locations.

ADA GUIDELINES

The Americans with Disabilities Act (ADA) has proposed a few guidelines regarding ATMs. Any new ATM installed after March 15, 2012, must comply with the ADA's rules and regulations. The purpose is to give people with disabilities equal access to public services. All ATMs must be accessible to people with disabilities, so specific accommodations are mandated. We've all seen braille ATM keypads on drive-up ATMs.

There is no way to get around these requirements. You have to comply with them to operate your ATM business legally. If you already own an ATM, you must ensure it meets these requirements. That means you need to make periodic adjustments to ensure you remain compliant as regulations change.

Remember that if the ATM provider gets named in a lawsuit and is sued because compliance is not met, the merchant (the location where the ATM is installed), most likely, is responsible and has a contractual agreement to indemnify the provider in the litigation. This is another reason that ATM paperwork is so necessary.

Listed below are the current ADA guidelines for ATMs:

Height & Reach

Reach refers to the height of the uppermost function key on the ATM machine. To ensure consumers can easily access input controls, an ATM's reach must be no higher than 48" from the ground. In 2012, the

ADA standards lowered ATM functions from 54", so you could come across older ATMs that don't meet this height and are still active and haven't been upgraded yet. Merchants and IADs sometimes push the limits and risk an ADA lawsuit by waiting longer than they should to update.

It is important to note that if the live touch-command areas on the ATM screen are higher than the function keys, the graphic area containing the touch commands must be lowered to the required height for the unit to comply.

Most freestanding retail ATM machines do not have touch screens yet and would, therefore, comply. However, as technology advances and future ADA updates are made, you must ensure you work with an ATM company that will keep you abreast of the changes. Drive-thru ATMs need not follow this regulation.

Now that it's been more than a decade, it's unlikely to encounter non-ADA compliant machines; however, if you see an ATM that is out of ADA compliance, it's an opportunity to let the merchant know.

ATM Area & Merchant Responsibility

There should be a floor space of 30 x 48 inches (10 sq. ft.) in front of the ATM to comply with the ADA wheelchair access guidelines.

The ADA requirements for ATMs pertain to the open floor space in front of an ATM. This is the responsibility of the property manager or merchant, regardless of the arrangement made with the IAD or other ATM provider. The merchant is responsible for ensuring the proper legal requirements for wheelchair access.

The minimum clear floor or ground space required for accommodating a single, stationary wheelchair and occupant is 30 in by 48 in (760 mm by 1220 mm).

Source: *http://www.ada.gov/regs2010/2010ADAStandards/2010ADAstandards.htm

Route

The entrance to the ATM must have a clear route leading up to it. This is to allow easy access for wheelchair-bound individuals.

Speech-Enabled Functionality, aka Voice Guidance

Every ATM machine in the United States must be speech-enabled for visually impaired customers. A 3.5mm female jack has to be installed in the ATM to allow the customers to use headphones.

The ADA considers speech output to be an auxiliary aid or service. Implementation is required only if doing so would create an undue burden or expense. Make sure when you purchase an ATM that it is a late model and meets this requirement.

Braille Instructions

The speech-enabled ATMs need to have instructions in Braille for visually-impaired customers to allow them to activate the voice feature. Most ATM companies include a welcome kit with ATM purchases that includes a Braille decal; however, most manufacturers have since included Braille on the machine surface. Since voice guidance can change depending on the ATM, if you receive a decal from your ATM company, be sure to place it on the machine near the audio jack.

Display Screen

The machine's display screen must be visible from 40 inches above the center of the floor in front of it. The font to be used for the text has to be Sans Serif. The font should contrast with the background and should be at least 3/16" high.

Since ATM manufacturers know these guidelines, you don't need to be concerned about them. However, you should still be aware of them.

Function Keys

The keys on the machine should be in a different color than the surface. The manufacturers know these guidelines and design the keys to contrast visually from their background surfaces.

All ATMs shipped to the United States for retail sale must have this configuration. Still, some older ATMs may have plastic keys and may not have the latest Visa Encrypting Pin Pad (VEPP keypad). PCI compliance is changing in 2025. All keypads will require an upgrade to a PCI compliant keypad, and the approved models vary by manufacturer. For Hyosung machines, you must have an 8000r or X1 model keypad. For Genmega machines, you must have a B3 or B5 model keypad. For Triton ATMs, you must have a T10 keypad. All new ATMs should already include these keypads. If you're not ordering ATMs from my firm, make sure when you place your equipment order that your ATMs will have the upgraded keypads already installed.

Input Devices

Customers should be able to discern the input devices. For this reason, the keys should be raised above the surface. All ATM manufacturers are also aware of this and design their machines accordingly.

Numeric Keys

The numeric layout of the keypad can be in either ascending or descending order. The Enter key should have a raised circle. The Clear key should have a raised left arrow indicating that pressing the key would erase what has been typed. The Add Value and Decrease Value keys should have plus and minus signs, respectively.

Suppose a location has more than one machine. In that case, the one most accessible from the entrance has to comply with the ADA guidelines. If there is one ATM inside a location and one outside, both have to be compliant. Only drive-thru ATMs are exempt from these guidelines. Also, they apply to all existing and new ATMs without exception.

If your ATMs don't comply with these regulations, you might have to bear a civil penalty which could be as high as $55,000, even for the first offense. The amount doubles for each subsequent offense.

You can ask your ATM provider to help you set up ATMs compliant with the ADA regulations so that you don't have to bear any legal hassle in the future. Also, providing services to disabled customers ensures that your machines get more transactions.

ATM SECURITY

Dial Tumbler Locks and e-Locks

A dial combo lock is the typical tumbler lock that comes on most safes and has tumblers where you turn the dial left three times, then right twice, then left once, then back again to open the safe. These locks are relatively standard and have been used for centuries. Yes, tumbler locks were used in ancient Egypt out of wood, then the Romans made them in iron.

The pros to these locks are that they are inexpensive and come standard on ATMs when you buy one. Dial combos come standard on many ATM machines.

The cons to these locks are that the combo is difficult to change and requires a change key that comes with the ATM. They take longer to open, and if you are loading an ATM during a busy day when the store is open, people can see what you are up to as it takes a few minutes to perfect.

An e-lock is an electronic lock upgrade. Some ATMs come with the e-lock, and some require an upgrade. When you order a new ATM, depending on the model, the upgrade to an e-lock is typically $50-$100, and it can be installed at the factory at no additional charge. If you wait to order one later or buy a used ATM with a standard dial combo and want to upgrade it to an e-lock, the cost could be $150 plus the price of a locksmith or an ATM field technician service call unless you are handy and can attempt it yourself. It's not difficult, just time-consuming, and requires the knowledge you can quickly learn.

E-locks are simple touch keypads that look similar to a telephone keypad. It takes less than a few seconds to enter the correct combination of keys and open your ATM.

While they offer easy, fast ATM access, they cost a little extra. I recommend spending a few extra dollars on the e-lock if you order a new ATM that does not include one. When you consider the total investment and the amount of time and hassle an e-lock saves, it's a no-brainer. If you plan to load several ATMs in one day, getting stuck for half an hour trying to open a dial lock sucks. The wasted time can make a huge difference if you're trying to finish loading before the store opens or if the owner is waiting for you.

A Kaba Mas or Cencon Lock is an electronic lock that includes the ability to assign special digital keys so you can perform a security audit. These locks are required when hiring an armored carrier for vault cash services. These locks tend to cost $500-$600 dollars each.

Cameras

Adding a camera to your ATM location is one of the easiest ways to secure it. Not only are cameras inconspicuous, but they provide a real-time feed of the location at which your ATM has been installed. Nothing deters thieves as much as being caught on camera. Having their faces recorded on video means they will get implicated if caught. The job of the law enforcement authorities is easier if they can see the face of the perpetrator.

The cost is the only reason people are apprehensive about adding cameras to their ATM locations. Cameras can be expensive, but they don't have to be. An indoor Blink or Ring camera can be connected to the merchant's Wi-Fi, and you can see it from your phone. If the merchant's ISP goes down, you have an issue, but a camera with its own communication can get expensive. Unless the machine has started generating revenue, making a further investment can be a problem for some new investors. It is another effective way to secure your investment, making it worthwhile.

What you can do is get a couple of web-ready cameras. For IADs whom I work with, we typically install a third-party camera system at the ATM locations: a two-camera system from Costco or any Ring Camera from Amazon (I don't mind Ring Refurbished cameras - see link in resources if you have print copy of the book) with one facing the ATM and one facing the entrance to the location. Then we add decals and on-screen graphics that say, "Smile, you're on camera." This does an excellent job of deterring any potential thieves.

Stolen ATMs

Not all ATM robberies are reported, but the percentage is meager compared to the number of ATMs in the United States. Most thieves don't know how much cash there is in a freestanding retail ATM. They check to see if they are bolted to the ground. Most thieves find it's not worth the risk. However, some still try since the advent of stronger battery-operated portable grinders and metal cutters.

To protect your investment, make your ATM less attractive to thieves. Bolt it down well. Use good hardware. Next, make sure the location has a monitored alarm system. Adding cameras, alarms, and other security measures is easy. Still, if you don't do anything, you risk your machine.

Plus, to protect yourself against the worst-case scenario, you can always opt to purchase insurance for your equipment and cash.

Additional Security Measures

Apart from adding the locks and cameras, there are a couple of other security measures you can put into place:

First, make sure the space around the machine is well-lit. The risk of theft and robbery is reduced when lights shine all around. That's one of the reasons people feel safer when using a well-lit ATM.

You can also ask the owner if you can provide and install an alarm at the location if the location doesn't already have one. Most thieves will avoid any store or location that is well-lit and has an alarm.

Install ATMs inside, away from large windows or glass doors whenever possible.

And try to select locations that have extended hours of operation. If the business is open 24 hours, that is the best type of location since there is constant surveillance and witnesses.

If you're a store owner with an ATM, and you or your managers are on-site, you can also make it a point to remove the cash from the machine every night. This is the same precaution you would take with your cash register.

Security is an extremely important issue when it comes to an ATM business. While there is a limited risk, you should also make customers comfortable using your ATM. Only then can you expect your business to grow and deliver the desired profits. Remember these security measures to help you run a successful ATM business. While insurance is not preventative and will add costs, it *can* give you peace of mind.

ATM INSURANCE

While ATM insurance is optional, without it, there is no protection from ATM losses for burglary, damage, or theft. Since you are independent of any banking institution, the FDIC won't cover you. But don't worry. ATM insurance is available and relatively affordable, but not for just one or two locations.

First of all, if you own your own store or business where you plan to install an ATM machine, check with your business insurance policy to see if you can add your ATM as an asset to be covered or add a rider (add-on) to your policy for special equipment. If you can't, or if your ATM is in a standalone location, you might want to consider purchasing ATM insurance.

While you can purchase insurance specific to ATM businesses (I provide resources for this at the end of the book), you can also look into a general liability policy. Business insurance is designed to protect your financial assets—all businesses face risks, and an ATM business is no exception. Therefore, as a business owner, the most comprehensive type of policy you can invest in is general liability insurance.

General liability coverage typically includes bodily injury, property damage, medical payments, and legal defense. Crime Coverage goes further to provide protection for the ATM funds, including situations of employee dishonesty, burglary, robbery, and property loss (removal/disappearance of the entire machine). Some ATM business insurance companies also offer Cash in Transit Coverage for protection when vaulting.

Here are some scenarios specific to your ATM business that would be covered (to some extent) by general liability insurance:

In the event of accidental damage to the location owner's property, while moving or installing the machine, insurance would cover replacement or repair. If a customer gets injured while using your ATM machine, insurance will cover the cost of treating the injury (I've never experienced this in 30 years). And if a disgruntled customer takes legal action against you or your company, insurance would cover the costs of defending yourself.

On the other hand, ATM business insurance is a little more specific than general liability insurance. General liability insurance might be the most common, most important, and bare minimum coverage you could consider. ATM insurance is written to cover potential loss and damage to your ATM machines and even the cash inside them. Like any other insurance policy, you purchase enough to cover your assets, so the premium amount depends on how much coverage you need, any riders you want, and any specific risks you want to mitigate.

Because of the risks associated with owning an ATM business, you might find that location owners will require you to carry liability insurance before they agree to work with you. So you might want to have this in place ahead of time in preparation for addressing this resistance. There are, of course, other ways to make sure you, your business, and your machine are protected. For example, you can write specific liability clauses in your contracts, add cameras to deter crime, and bolt down the machine during installation. Don't be surprised if insurance companies require some of these actions as a condition of coverage.

When purchasing insurance for your ATM business, be sure to double-check which scenarios are covered and which aren't. If you want more coverage than what's offered, see if it can be added if it falls within your budget. Liability insurance is not expensive, but it may not necessarily be required either, so check with your city. It also depends on your level of risk and if you have anything worth insuring yet.

TRAINING AND OPERATION

Using an ATM machine to perform a transaction as a customer and operating it as the owner is very different. Just because you've used an ATM before doesn't mean you will automatically know how to operate one. There are several functions you have to master before you can run an ATM machine as a successful business.

Learning the Functions

While it is easier to load an ATM machine than a cash register and even a napkin holder, proper training and experience can help you avoid costly mistakes.

Even if you are not the one who is going to be physically operating the machine and loading the cash, it is imperative that you understand how the process works. Eventually, you may have to train someone else to do the job for you. Second, you may have to operate the machine if the other person is unavailable. This is why it's important to learn the different functions of the various ATM machines you own.

The great thing about modern ATMs is that the operating system is Windows-based. If you've used smartphones or tablets, know what menus are, etc., it's familiar in a way. ATMs are fully functional and programmed to make it convenient for the owner to operate them. You will receive an owner's manual with each machine you purchase. However, even if you consult the manual, it is quite possible that you might need a more in-depth understanding at times. So, what do you do in that situation?

Where to Get Training for Operating Your ATM

Your best option is to get professional training for operating the ATM. Having someone teach you how to work the actual machine is often better than reading about it and then trying it. (Personally, I'm a hands-on learner.) This is not to say it can't be done, but getting professional experience is always better than trial and error. This is why it is important that you take some time and receive proper training. When I got trained, the ATM manufacturers required you to fly to Texas for a 2-day in-depth training course. That's not required these days.

The great thing about this business is that most ATM providers offer training services. When you order an ATM, ask if the company provides training. If they do, ask them how the training takes place. Do you need to travel to a special office? Does someone come to you during installation? Can it be done over the phone, online, etc.? There are many options. Ideally, you should get hands-on training done during the first ATM installation. This way, you will be completely adept and familiar with the workings of the ATM machine you own. You can practically guarantee that there will be no downtime for your machines if you are properly trained to handle any issues.

The best ATM providers don't charge extra for training if it's done during the installation process. While the machine is being installed and programmed to bring it into working condition, you can be taught the various functions of the machine. The installer will cover every aspect of the machine you need to know to operate it successfully.

To make the most of your ATM business, it is imperative that your machines are up and running all of the time. For that, you need to understand what to check and when, as well as any necessary actions that are required if there is an issue. So get in touch with your ATM provider and discuss the training process.

I recommend hiring a field technician the first time and letting the tech install it, program it, and give you some training while you record it on your phone for future reference. Then, subsequent ATMs you can have preprogrammed by the manufacturer if you don't have the time or inclination to do that part, but you can bolt it in yourself or hire a local handyman.

REVENUE AND FEES

This is perhaps the most relevant of all topics covered in this book. Setting up an ATM business aims to build wealth, earn a nice passive income, work fewer hours than a full-time job, and get a much higher annual return from cash than money just sitting in a bank account.

Regarding revenue from your ATM business, it will most likely be in the form of transaction fees. The customers who use your machine will be charged a fee for each transaction they perform using your machine. The more transactions you generate and the more customers you can attract, the greater your revenue will be. This transaction fee is known as the surcharge.

Surcharge Fee

You will hear many people question why they must pay a surcharge to access their cash from an ATM. The answer to that is quite simple: convenience. Customers can travel to their bank to get money from a teller or locate one of their bank's ATMs. While these are great choices for consumers, people are busy, find they are short on cash, and it's inconvenient to locate an ATM from their bank.

Your ATM machine offers consumers a convenient option. For this convenience, they are charged a fee. This is especially necessary since you must invest in the equipment and keep it loaded with cash. In reality, an ATM is simply a cash-dispensing vending machine. It's the same concept as the additional cost of getting sodas or snacks from machines. It's convenient, and someone has to own and load the machines.

While banks do not usually charge a surcharge fee on their ATMs for their own customers (some virtual banks without ATMs also reimburse surcharge fees to their customers), non-banking customers will typically be charged.

However, you will be a private ATM owner, and one of the ways you will make money is through the surcharge fee. You can set the fee according to your preference. Typically, the surcharge fee falls between $1.00 and $8.00. Fees vary due to many factors. The average fee nationwide is about $2.95; however, some large financial institutions are now charging $3.50 to non-bank customers. To determine the best surcharge for your machine, visit the competition in the area where you plan to install the machine to set a competitive surcharge. Speak with your ATM company representative until you are comfortable and have the experience necessary to maximize your revenue.

Remember that there are a few costs associated with owning and operating an ATM that your revenue will have to cover. The machine will be the highest cost, which will cost between $2,000 and $5,000 or more, depending on the model and features needed, until you make your ROI. Other costs include maintenance, service, receipt paper, communications, loading and reloading costs (gas and travel time), etc. While there are electricity costs, these are typically minimal and paid by the location owner. How much electricity? Very little. When it's idle, which is 99% of the time, it uses about 25 watts. To put that in comparison, an average TV uses about 200 watts, and an outdoor bug bulb is 60 watts. You have to cover these costs and make a profit, and charging a surcharge fee is the best way, but not the only way.

You can increase or decrease the surcharge fee with your ATM provider at any time; however, fees could be associated with that process. You'll soon determine the best fee for each machine to maximize your revenue.

Interchange

Interbank fees, or interchange, refer to the money card networks pay to have transactions made on your ATM machine routed through them. When you have your ATM machine installed and programmed, your ATM processor connects your machine to the networks that pay them interchange to route transactions through them. Since these transactions are made using your machine, you can sometimes get a share of that interchange fee if you have enough transactions and are willing to pay transaction fees and other costs. If you're just starting out and need a lot of help, you often won't qualify to receive interchange because it goes toward the cost of the service you receive from the ATM processing company. They have to make money to service you.

ISOs sometimes pay IADs part of this interchange if the total number of transactions outweighs the costs of managing your accounts. The revenue that can be made from interchange is based on the network the transactions ride on and volume. The networks like Visa (Plus) and MasterCard (Cirrus) have various levels of interchange charged to the card issuer (the bank that issued the card) and then, what they share with the processor is based on the type of transaction (inquiry, denial, withdrawal, international transaction, and others).

The more transactions the ISO processes for you and the less support you need, the more money they can typically pass on to you. Therefore, the interchange is a way for IADs to make additional revenue per transaction once your volume and experience warrant it.

Some processors use preferential routing—this could be based on local networks or networks that pay higher interchange rates—to help their IADs make more interchange revenue.

Very experienced ATM business operators can often get a buy rate for transaction processing. This happens when you have a lot of transactions; you'd need at least ten thousand transactions per month or more to participate where it makes sense. In this situation, when IADs get a buy rate, it means you pay the transaction fees and are charged every time your ATM connects with the processor. It also means you don't rely on much phone support when buying, installing, and managing your ATM business.

A good ATM provider will be transparent about fees and revenue and should disclose everything upfront. Unfortunately, not all will. So it's important that you talk to your ATM provider about their fee structure. ISOs have their own costs to cover and are for-profit businesses also, so if you receive a buy rate or share in the interchange, be prepared to pay some type of transaction fee (usually deducted from the interchange) with the remainder passed on to you.

Interchange is the fee banks have to pay the networks like Plus, Cirrus, STAR, NYCE, etc. for routing the transactions to the appropriate account for out-of-network transactions. When you use your bank's ATM machine, they know your account information and usually do not have to route your ATM transaction through a third-party network. These transactions stay in-house or in-network and usually do not require the bank to pay interchange fees.

Interchange is only paid on out-of-network transactions. Since your ATM will always be out of the customer's network (unless you make deals with local and regional banks and need BIN blocking), the customer's bank will have to pay the interchange.

Customers will often get charged a bank fee for using an out-of-network ATM in addition to the surcharge. (Several online banks offer ATM reimbursement of some or all of these fees to their customers.) Usually, local, regional, and some national banks charge customers to encourage them to use in-network ATMs.

However, when bank customers have to perform ATM transactions urgently or conveniently and select an out-of-network ATM, the only option for that ATM is to perform an out-of-network transaction. In that case, the customer may also be charged an out-of-network fee by their bank, which most likely pays various network fees.

This means that the customer's bank is paying the network and the ATM processing company to enable him or her to perform the withdrawal or any other transaction on out-of-network ATMs.

ATM companies are not obligated to divulge details regarding the interchange being paid by the bank. However, if you have a large portfolio of ATMs or are building your ATM business and processing tens of thousands of transactions monthly, it could mean you are missing out on some of the additional revenue. These types of companies may try to hide the interchange, charge you erroneous fees, and not care if your ATM business makes money.

Before surcharging, the interchange was the only way banks were compensated for letting non-account holders use their ATMs. Also, remember that commercial ATMs that banks install can cost ten to twenty times more than the machines private ATM owners like you deploy.

Each network has different interchange rates, structures, and tiers. Interchange has been evolving and is typically how ATM processing companies, ISOs, bank sponsors, and other entities involved in the business get paid.

Some ATM companies will share some of the interchange with IADs, depending on the volume of transactions. Some ATM companies also offer pass-through pricing, known as a flat rate, buy rate, or net rate pricing. This is typically done for an ISO.

This is where they pass on the entire surcharge and the interchange to the ISO and then simply charge one flat fee for each transaction plus bank sponsorship. If you build up your ATM business to the point where you are processing tens of thousands of ATM transactions, the ATM company you work with may offer pass-through pricing once you learn the business, have enough transactions, and take on additional responsibilities to warrant that rate structure.

Again, this comes down to the provider you select. You should ensure that the ATM provider you select is reliable, reputable, and has long been in the business so that your residuals are never at risk.

Processing Fees

You earn revenue from surcharges and interchange (if you participate), and you could, in turn, be charged fees known as driving, transaction, or processing fees. I call them processing fees. They are charged on every transaction if you have buy-rate pass-through pricing.

Some providers charge other types of fees depending on the cards used in your ATM if you're sharing in the interchange. These fees are often small charges that vary from $0.01 to $0.18 (as of the writing of this book) and come from a variety of different networks or processors that tack on a fee since interchange has been going down and other expenses are going up. The only way for them to make money is to charge the fees (pass-through) being reduced or deducted.

As previously discussed, the networks typically charge issuer and acquirer fees to the bank that issued the ATM card.

MasterCard, for example, imposes its service and other fees against the interchange and pays the difference to the ATM processor. Beginning April 2010, MasterCard implemented a tiered system that now charges its card-issuing bank different amounts based on transaction volume.

MasterCard imposes its fees against these tiered amounts. This means the net interchange paid by MasterCard might be as low as $0.15 per ATM transaction, depending on the transaction volume of the card-issuing bank. This can change at the network's will.

MasterCard's April 2010, pricing change affected each ATM withdrawal involving a U.S.-issued card used at an ATM located in the United States. MasterCard charges a $0.05 Program Support Fee on each ATM withdrawal and a variable Brand Volume Fee of 0.095% of the amount withdrawn to the ATM acquirer. Both of these fees are subtracted from the net interchange. Beginning April 2010, the Program Support Fee increased from $0.05 to $0.18 for each withdrawal, and the Brand Volume Fee was eliminated. The result is that lower-volume ATM deployers are often seeing this $0.18 fee coming out of their revenue.

Visa followed suit and also added a similar acquirer fee to Visa-surcharged transactions, as did several other networks, including PULSE, NYCE, and a few others. Some ATM companies have charged a flat fee to eliminate accounting and statement nightmares between reporting networks.

PULSE, a Discover Financial Services Company subsidiary, also announced a pricing change effective May 1, 2010. For all U.S.-approved and declined ATM cash withdrawals and cash advances, PULSE now charges a fee called the U.S. ATM Acquirer Fee of $0.03. This fee is in addition to PULSE's existing ATM Network Security Fee of $0.01, applied to all U.S. and international approved and declined ATM cash withdrawals and cash advances.

Keep in mind that the network charges the fees, so if you're working with an ATM provider that offers priority routing, connecting your ATMs to local and regional networks whenever possible, your fees may vary when you are on a flat rate or buy rate. Or, if you share part of the interchange, some fees may be passed through.

It's all based on the ATM cards inserted by your customers and the routing from your ATM provider. The ATM company I work with uses priority routing and tries to avoid fees or keep them to a minimum whenever possible. These fees involving pennies per transaction often occur on surcharged transactions only. So, if you get buy rate pricing, your surcharge and additional interchange easily offset any network fee.

Surcharge, interchange, acquirer, sponsorship, processing, driving, and other fees are the main types of fees you need to know about when projecting the revenue for your ATM business.

Your customers have to pay you for using your machine. The surcharge is where the bulk of your income will be derived from. If you receive any interchange income, it is often used to offset any fees. Depending on the network usage, these fees can reduce your monthly revenue, but only slightly. Suppose you are getting some portion of the interchange fee and being charged other fees. In that case, it can often be a wash and will probably not affect your monthly revenue if you base it only on the surcharge amount. Then you can ignore all the fees and focus on surcharge revenue.

Many processors and ISOs will offer you 100% of your surcharge and not charge you any of the network fees if you want to keep it simple. That way, if you have slow ATMs during certain times of the year (seasonal machines) or when your ATM is just starting to ramp up, it can take a few months before it reaches a good transaction level where your fees are close to interchange. As a brand new IAD, don't expect to share in the interchange right away anyway. I just use the surcharge as the revenue projection to keep it simple.

BANK NETWORKS

As previously mentioned, your ATMs will be connected to a processing provider that will connect your ATM with the proper networks in order to be operational. There is no way you can get your machines up and running if they aren't connected to a network. So you need to understand what interbank networks are.

Interbank Networks

Many people no longer withdraw cash by making a trip to the bank. They find the nearest ATM and perform all of their transactions there or online. What is amazing about ATM technology is that customers can withdraw money from a machine even if it isn't owned and operated by their bank.

This is where interbank networks are at work. The interbank networks allow people to withdraw cash from any machine on the network regardless of the bank where they keep their money. The interbank network is what allows customers to perform the transactions they do on ATM machines. The interesting thing is that few, if any, users actually know what goes into performing an ATM transaction.

Several interbank networks are currently in operation, including Plus, Cirrus, PULSE, AFFN, and STAR, along with a host of other networks. When a customer conducts a transaction on the machine, the machine relays the relevant information to the customer's bank. The information then attributes the transaction to the customer's account.

The machines themselves are connected through a controller. Nowadays, most retail ATM machines utilize a high-speed internet connection or a wireless device. This ensures that their customers get to enjoy speedy service and keep coming back to use the machine.

Customers can still perform out-of-network transactions on the ATMs near them. However, sometimes, the fee charged is higher than that of an in-network ATM. This is why most people prefer to withdraw cash from an ATM machine operated by their bank.

There are two main types of interbank networks: regional and national.

Regional Networks and National Networks

As an ATM business owner, you should know the difference between the two types of networks so that you can ask the right questions when selecting an ATM provider.

Regional networks typically work on ATM cards from regional banks. They can also be utilized by national banks, though this happens less often.

Regional networks include STAR and NYCE, for example, while national networks include Plus (owned by Visa) and Cirrus (owned by MasterCard).

Customers banking with a regional bank may see the logo of a regional network on the back of their ATM cards while customers of national banks will often see the logos of national networks.

National networks span the entire country while regional networks are located in specific areas of the U.S.

If you bank with a small community bank that only offers regional network access and you travel to another area of the country or to another country, you may not be able to find an ATM that offers that network. However, most ATM providers now offer all-network access. The key is to find an ATM provider that offers access to the most networks and smart or priority transaction routing to the most profitable network available for each ATM card.

BENEFITS OF ATMS

We rarely think about having to run to the bank to get cash. Many of us take it for granted that any time we are outdoors and run out of cash, we can simply visit the nearest ATM and withdraw the amount we need. You only need to have your ATM card, and you are good to go. This is a great option for people who don't like carrying too much cash. Plus, it offers a cushion in case you run out of cash while shopping or purchasing something expensive.

Undoubtedly, people have become accustomed to and dependent on ATMs, and it would be difficult for individuals to conduct commerce without them. And ATMs benefit businesses as well.

You can make a steady income operating an ATM business. It is a lucrative industry and offers plenty of opportunities for success.

Most business owners don't have any idea how valuable having an ATM on the premises can be. This is why some business owners don't think about having one installed, or they are just too busy to take the time to understand the principles of ATM benefits. And there are numerous benefits to owning and operating an ATM business.

BENEFITS OF ATMS FOR RETAIL BUSINESS OWNERS

Business owners in the retail sector can benefit from having an ATM in their stores. Retail stores with an ATM on site make more sales and are more successful. The most significant reason for this is that people must come in to use the ATM. Since they are in the store and withdrawing cash, they often end up buying small items or impulse items.

In fact, simply notifying people that you have an ATM on your premises can increase the foot traffic in your store. More people coming in means more customers. It is up to you to determine how you are going to convert ATM users into customers. Otherwise, it is pretty much a given that more people will enter your store once you hang a sign outside advertising you have an ATM in your store.

There are also psychological factors to consider. When people have money in their pockets, which they do after performing an ATM transaction, they tend to buy on impulse. There are few opportunities for businesses to trigger the impulse buying reaction of their patrons. With an ATM, store owners can get more people to shop without having to use any marketing gimmicks.

You need to be shrewd with the placement of your ATM. If you have it set up right next to the bargain counter, it is possible that you might be able to increase your sales substantially. A small retail business could generate hundreds of dollars in additional profits on a weekly basis simply by installing an ATM.

The most significant advantage is for businesses that operate on a cash basis as well as those whose employees expect tips. This goes for any retail business, small or large. Customers prefer to pay with cash than with credit cards, so encouraging cash payments lowers credit card processing fees. Since customers can withdraw cash at the store, merchants benefit by avoiding the credit card processing fee. Plus, by paying with cash instead of credit cards, customers don't have to accumulate debt every time they go shopping. The other advantage is when it's an establishment where customers are used to tipping. Cash tipping is much preferred and will make employees much happier. Happy employees often mean better customer service, which can translate to good reviews and word-of-mouth advertising. There are many hidden benefits to having an ATM available.

ATM customers might also look to break a large bill. To do that, they would be forced to buy from you. Large retail stores might not be too impressed by this, but installing an ATM could make a huge difference to a small business's revenue.

In any case, you receive a surcharge fee when people use your ATM, even if they don't buy anything. So it's a win-win situation.

All in all, installing an ATM at a business location is a great opportunity for the business owner. Not only is the business likely to attract more customers, but it also makes money from the fees being charged for ATM transactions and can reduce other payment form expenses as well as other hidden benefits.

BENEFITS OF OWNING AND OPERATING AN ATM BUSINESS

The income you generate from your ATM business is the foremost advantage. The fact that you have little to do to keep your machine(s) up and running makes it mostly a passive income business. The ATM company you work with will help you set up and program the machine. You don't even have to be physically present at the location unless the ATM is installed on your business premises.

The capital outlay for an ATM business is also limited. You only need to invest in the machines, which you can buy on credit if necessary. There are no major operating costs. The income from the daily transactions on your ATM should easily cover the overhead. You can set up a full-fledged ATM business, installing five or six machines for under $25,000, including the equipment cost and enough cash to start loading. If you want to get a business equipment loan from a bank or line of credit for the equipment, then you only need cash for your money inventory.

The income from just five or six ATMs in an average location (about five transactions per day) would be between $1,500 and $2,500 per month (depending on your surcharge, who is vaulting, and any revenue shared with the location owner). Obviously, the income from busier ATM locations is going to be much higher.

Even though there are close to 500,000 ATMs already operational across the United States, there are still plenty of locations where there is demand and need for an ATM. So there are perfectly viable opportunities for you to take advantage of and set up your ATM business.

Last but not least, it is highly unlikely that the demand for ATMs will fall in the near future. More people have begun to realize the fact that withdrawing cash and performing transactions on ATMs is safe and reliable. Therefore, demand is on the rise. So you can expect a steady number of transactions per day at the right locations. With time, you will realize the scope of your business and decide whether or not you want to expand.

Those are the benefits of owning and operating an ATM business. It has been a great business for me since 1994. It continues to generate passive income for anyone involved nationwide. The only potential drawback of starting an ATM business is the risk of installing an ATM in a low-performing location. However, even the slowest locations return an annual percentage far exceeding what you would get from saving money in a local bank account or CD.

Even if you install an ATM in a location that only produces forty transactions monthly (that's just over 1 transaction per day), at a $3.00 surcharge, you still earn upwards of a 50% annualized return on your investment, and that's if the ATM is in a terrible location.

Let's do the math—forty transactions at $3 equals $120 monthly. Twelve months in the year is $1440 gross revenue. A $2,500 investment in equipment with normal business depreciation, less any costs for gas or bank fees, should still net you close to $1,250 in profit, which is a 50% annualized return. Even if you only net $100 a month, and it takes 25 months to ROI the equipment, your business has a depreciating asset on the books, which will still be worth more than $1,000 once you fully depreciate it. You'd also make $1200 a year or more with company assets.

If this is a risk you are willing to take, this business is for you. If you follow the tips and advice in this book, you shouldn't have any trouble making your ATM business profitable.

OPPORTUNITIES IN THE ATM BUSINESS

While owning and operating the ATMs yourself will result in the most income if you don't have the funds to start by owning your own ATMs, there are many other ways to earn a passive income in the ATM business.

Become an ATM Site Locator

Several ATM business opportunities don't require a capital investment (buying machines or loading cash). One of the opportunities is to become an ATM site locator.

An ATM site locator is a person who finds the locations that are interested in having an ATM in or at their location. This could be a retail store, a commercial building, a manufacturing facility, a strip mall, a parking lot, or bank branding opportunities.

You could be the one who finds out who the right person is to talk to and then negotiate terms as if you were placing your own machine. Then, work with an ATM company to have another IAD put his or her ATM in that location. You also have to find out who will load the cash (it could be the ATM owner, the location, or another third party if you don't have funds for vaulting).

Suffice it to say, however, the more the site locator does, the more he or she can earn. For example, if you found a good location, and the owner of the location also didn't want to make the capital investment in the hardware but was willing to load the cash, you could theoretically share the surcharge three ways: the hardware owner, the location for loading the cash, and you for finding the location and making the deal.

There are many ways to make a deal work; learning the lingo and what makes it a win-win for everyone is vital to making the right deal. This is an example of how to enter the passive income ATM business without purchasing your own ATMs.

Obviously, if you have the cash and found a good location, you would want to install your own machine to maximize your revenue, but if you want to start slow, want to leverage existing relationships to get many locations quickly, do not have $25,000 in a bank account to support ten locations, or just need help from an ISO or IAD, you can still get some passive income going. Eventually, you will have the funds to add machines to your own portfolio.

Sell the ATM and Service to the Location

Sometimes, a location owner does not want someone to put an ATM in their place of business or another location. They may prefer to operate the ATM themselves and reap the associated rewards.

In this case, you can sell the location owner the ATM hardware (with a small markup for a commission) and provide a monthly maintenance agreement as your passive income. While it may not be as much and nearly as lucrative as getting the surcharge, your risk is completely removed. Remember the old adage, "The greater the risk, the greater the reward." While owning and loading an ATM is not very risky, it is obviously a lot less risky to not do anything and still earn some income for maintenance. You can offer cleaning services, paper replenishment, and monthly preventative maintenance (cleaning dispenser rollers, card reader cleaners, and even sell ad screens if the merchant approves).

Load the Cash (Vaulting)

This is another easy way to enter the ATM business. If you don't want to negotiate with location owners or service ATMs yourself but live in an area where you see a lot of ATMs, you can offer a cash-loading service (especially if you see "Out of Order" signs often).

You can also contact ATM companies and tell them that you are a private ATM vaulter. Come up with a schedule of fees based on the distance to a location. Sometimes, a vaulter can make $0.50 or $1.00 per transaction or more, depending on how busy the location is, how much cash the ATM goes through, and if they provide any other associated services (paper replacement, card reader cleaning, device cleaning, paper jams, journal reports, etc.).

Some ATM companies seek out vaulters when off-site deployers prefer not to pay for an armored car service for locations where that service can't be justified due to the added expense.

Independent Sales Organization (ISO)

ISOs are typically large organizations that file reams of paperwork and pay expensive annual fees in order to be registered with the networks and sponsor banks directly. This route is only advisable if you plan to process over a million transactions monthly or are well on your way. Otherwise, the fees, time, and resources required to be an ISO outweigh the gains of operating as an IAD.

ISOs are held to strict standards for securing master keys, complying with audits, having the required insurance, and making sure all their sub-ISOs abide by their rules. They are required to conform to the processor and sponsor bank standards and must comply with all network regulations. They also don't typically get much of a discount on ATMs unless they commit to purchasing 500-2,000 or more machines annually.

Subcontracted Independent Sales Organization (Sub-ISO)

This is an ISO-approved organization. Sub-ISOs partner with the ISO and typically have to process a minimum required number of monthly transactions, follow network master key rules, and be approved by the sponsor bank. Sub-ISOs often manage a fleet of their own ATMs, as well as manage IAD portfolios.

BITCOIN

I'm sure you've heard a ton about Bitcoin and that it's a form of cryptocurrency (digital money) that can be used to make local and international purchases.

Bitcoin can be bought, sold, and traded. This is where Bitcoin ATMs (BTMs) come in. BTMs are very similar to the regular ATMs you are familiar with. This is one of the reasons they are quickly rising in popularity: the simplicity lessens the apprehension of users new to cryptocurrency. This is also good news for you because if you get the regular ATM business down, the learning curve is relatively small if you decide to transition to BTMs or use software to make your ATM work as a BTM too. (As of this writing, stand-alone BTMs are much more expensive than an ATM with BTM software.)

One of the main differences between these two businesses is demand. The BTM business will be more niche than a regular ATM business. This means you will be more limited in successfully operating a dedicated BTM. You'll have to look for locations with large populations of crypto users to make it worthwhile. And depending on where you live, this just might not be an option.

There are two types of BTMs: one-way and two-way. One-way BTMs allow users to purchase Bitcoin or Alternate coins (alt-coins). Bitcoin can be purchased from a BTM machine with cash or debit card, and the Bitcoin can be sent to any wallet users choose, whether their own or someone else's. This versatility adds to the convenience of BTM machines.

Two-way BTMs allow users to both buy *and* sell Bitcoin. While users can withdraw cash from their bank accounts at a regular ATM, they can sell their Bitcoin in exchange for cash at a BTM. BTMs do not connect to bank accounts but to digital wallets. They also connect to digital token exchanges, which are digital marketplaces for buying and selling bitcoin.

Another benefit of BTMs is that the trading process happens in a matter of seconds rather than days when compared to exchange websites which sometimes impose minimum purchase limits as well.

The process for starting a stand-alone Bitcoin ATM business is similar to that of a regular ATM business, with several caveats and options:

1. Get compliant with paperwork.
2. Purchase equipment or work as a referral agent.
3. Find a location.
4. Supply Bitcoin unless you work with or under an MSB (MSBs supply BTC).
5. Start making money.

Get Compliant with Paperwork

To legally operate a stand-alone BTM, you may have to register yourself as a money services business (MSB) with the U.S. Treasury's Financial Crimes Enforcement Network (FinCEN). You will also need to register for an Anti-Money Laundering (AML) program. This can affect your ATM business bank account, so be sure to get that setup first if you plan to operate both businesses.

AML programs are required to help prevent money laundering practices via BTM. Not all AML programs look the same. Certain requirements exist, but you can have a program custom-built to meet your business needs.

Another regulation feature is Know Your Customer (KYC) verification. KYC verification decreases fraudulent BTM activity by identifying users and flagging suspicious activity.

You might also need a money transmitter license. Depending on where your BTM is located, you might be required to adjust the limits on deposits and withdrawals. You can always check with a professional like your provider to ensure you are fully compliant.

Purchase Equipment

All of the tips I provided for purchasing ATM equipment apply to BTM equipment. One-way machines (approx. $3,500) and ATM sidecars (Hyosung) will run less than two-way machines (approx. $6,500). Choose a machine that meets your business needs and the needs of the users in your area. Many ATM providers can also help you convert your existing or new ATM into a dual-use BTM/ATM and save you all the trouble of registering as an MSB. An ATM company familiar with Hyosung Bitcoin sidecars and kiosks can help you do this.

Security features like locks and cameras are recommended, but they are additional features that you can add at any time. Consider things like backup battery, bill capacity, and warranty. You also have a number of options when it comes to the interface. Do you want users to sign in with a QR code, thumbprint, or handprint scan?

Most importantly, you want to make sure you purchase your BTM equipment from a provider that is going to work with you throughout the entire process. Small and new manufacturers are introducing many BTMs. Be careful. A good ATM/BTM equipment provider will be available to answer your questions and assist whenever needed.

If you are already working with an ATM provider or want to go that route first, you can ask whether they offer BTM services. Most Hyosung ATMs can be upgraded with Bitcoin capabilities, saving you time and money later.

Find a Location

As I mentioned, there is a narrower market for BTMs than ATMs. Specifically, you're looking for areas with high populations of Bitcoin users and cryptocurrency enthusiasts.

As of this printing, the average cryptocurrency user is 38 years old, and most users are male. However, millennials are increasingly becoming the majority of crypto investors. So look for locations that serve these groups: bars, coffee shops, gentlemen's clubs, etc.

This doesn't mean that these are the only potentially profitable locations. Since younger generations are likely to be more confident traders of cryptocurrency, universities and surrounding areas are good ideas too.

Finally, although a small percentage of Americans own cryptocurrency, many are curious. In the near future, we could see more BTMs in places like restaurants, shopping centers, and salons serving a more diverse population. I think we are several years away from profitable BTMs. Still, if you start in the ATM business now and learn it, you will be ready to venture into BTMs as it gains popularity.

And again, the same placement strategy applies to BTMs as to ATMs: look for places with heavy foot traffic and businesses that are interested in lowering their credit card transaction fees. You might find some locations that already accept Bitcoin payments or some that are willing to start. These are good incentives to mention when proposing a placement agreement with store owners.

Supply Bitcoin

You will need a large investment if you decide to go the full MSB route. Plan to invest at least a few hundred thousand. It is expensive to become an MSB, and you will need to inventory enough Bitcoin to satisfy demand.

There are three ways to supply your customers with Bitcoin (BTC):

First, you can purchase large amounts of Bitcoin from exchange websites like Coinbase.com using your bank account or debit card. The currency gets added to your digital wallet, and customers can then purchase Bitcoin back from you through the BTM.

Second, you can purchase Bitcoin from another individual. You pay cash, and he or she transfers Bitcoin to your wallet.

Third, you can recycle the coin. This will be easier to do once you've been in operation for a while. You won't be able to choose this method for start-up, but this happens when one customer sells Bitcoin for cash, and then that Bitcoin is purchased by the next. So you build a repository of coins from users who sell you their BTC using your machine to get paid, then other users buy the BTC from your machine.

Start Making Money

BTM transaction fees are different from ATM surcharges. ATM surcharges are a set rate per transaction. BTM transaction fees are a percentage of the transaction amount. Not only this, but BTM transaction rates fluctuate constantly. Because of the constant variations and shifts in Bitcoin, you'll need to check a website like Cryptofees.net daily to find the current average transaction fee amount.

Then, just like operating an ATM, you'll want to charge a percentage that balances your desired income and convenience for your users.

In all honesty, I didn't go through becoming an MSB. It's just too expensive, stand-alone BTMs are still very risky, and the ROI can take many years. I convert ATMs to dual-use ATMs/BTM in locations that make sense. Not many do yet, as digital currency adoption is relatively new.

CONCLUSION

Congratulations. You kept your promise to yourself and read to the end of the book. By now, you should know what to expect when setting up an ATM business and have a clear idea of what is required to set up your ATM business.

When you go through the book in order, it covers the pertinent information you need to understand the ATM business. Now it's up to you to put what you have learned into action.

Here's a recap:

- The basics of an ATM business, including what it is and how it works
- How to choose a location for placing an ATM
- How do you make money?
- Your role and responsibility
- Who installs and programs the machines?
- Who loads and reloads the machines?
- Which machines are the best?
- How do you arrange the cash to load into the machines?
- Learning to operate the machine
- The different revenue streams you can set up
- Security features you can add to your ATM locations
- Optional hardware for your machines

I have tried to be as detailed as possible, given that the average person doesn't know much about ATMs or ATM businesses. This is why each chapter is quite comprehensive in scope and includes anything even remotely relevant to running an ATM business. I aim to educate you about establishing an ATM business and how to make it successful.

Surprisingly, ATMs are everywhere. Yet, only a few people actually think of making a living through them. After reading this book, you can.

The only requirement for you is to follow the tips and procedures provided. If you do so, you should have no problem setting up an ATM business and making it successful.

I wish you all of the success in the world, and should you want to get your business up and running or already have a location in mind, please visit the resource section for the next steps or call my company.

GLOSSARY

ACH - Automated Clearing House. A network that processes electronic financial transactions.

Acquirer fees - Fees imposed by the networks to the bank or financial institution that issued the ATM card. The network acquires the transaction on behalf of the issuing bank and charges a fee depending on the network that acquired the transaction.

Americans with Disabilities Act (ADA) - A 1990 civil rights law that gives people with disabilities equal access to public services by mandating certain accommodations.

Armored car service/armored carrier - A cash transport service that secures the cash in a guarded, monitored vehicle.

ATM card - A payment card issued by a bank that can be used to access financial accounts through an ATM. Often an ATM card is the same as a debit card but different from a credit card.

ATM display - Screen on the ATM that shows transaction and account details and ads if applicable.

ATM management - Service that handles an ATM's installation, cash loading, and maintenance.

ATM network - Channel that facilitates interbank communication so that a customer can use his or her bank card at another bank's ATM.

ATM owner - The individual (entrepreneur), group of individuals, or company that purchases an ATM, operates it, and receives most of the profits made through the machine.

ATM placement - Arrangement where an ATM company or IAD places an ATM in a location and owns and operates all aspects of the ATM. The location owner receives a small percentage of the revenue generated from the ATM in return for letting the IAD place the ATM at the location.

ATM processor - ATM vendor---or company---that sells and provides support for ATMs.

ATM processing - Communication between an ATM and a processing network that communicates with the user's bank to route financial transactions.

ATM service provider - ATM processor or ATM vendor that sells machines and is responsible for providing ongoing support regarding the operation of the machines.

ATM vaulter - The person who loads the ATM with cash.

ATM vendor - A company that sells and supports ATMs and/or ATM services to other ATM Businesses.

Bill dispenser/presenter - Cash dispensing mechanism that dispenses or presents the cash to customers.

BIN (blocking) - Bank Identification Number. The first six digits of a bank card number identify the bank that issued the card. BIN blocking is when the ATM processor blocks a bank's BIN (the bank-issued cards) from being surcharged.

Bitcoin - A decentralized digital currency (cryptocurrency) that can be sent from user to user without a central bank.

Capital outlay - The costs associated with acquiring an asset.

Cash loader - Person or party responsible for refilling cash in an ATM.

Cash run rate - How long your vault cash lasts; the rate at which your vault cash is withdrawn.

Cash settlement policy - A schedule ATM providers use for funds being returned to the settlement account.

Cassette - The box in an ATM holds a specific cash denomination.

CDU - Cash Dispensing Unit

Commercial - Commerce designed for and targeted to a large market.

Communications - Systems, devices, and/or a process that entails exchanging digital or spoken information.

Controller - System used to route financial transactions between ATMs and banks.

Credit card processing fee - Typically, a percentage plus flat fee merchants pay credit card processors per credit or debit card transaction. Rates vary by processor.

DBA - Doing business as. The name used for your business to avoid conducting business under your own name. See FBN.

Denominations - The seven types of paper currency ($1, $2, $5, $10, $20, $50, $100) available in the United States.

Diminishing returns - Receipt of smaller profits or benefits after investing more money or energy.

Dip reader - Document Insertion Processor. A device that reads data encoded on a magnetic stripe or computer chip on a debit or credit card.

Dispenser - A mechanism that issues bills one at a time into a tray upon approval from an ATM user. In contrast, a Presenter presents the bills all at the same time.

Downtime - Period when an ATM is inoperable.

Drop safe - A depository safe. Deposits can be inserted through a slot in the safe and, once inside, are secured and protected from theft.

E-lock - An electronic lock that is operated by an electric current.

Europay, MasterCard, and Visa (EMV) - Payment methods are made more secure using a computer chip embedded in the card. These chips can be used in payment terminals and ATMs that accept them or are EMV enabled.

Fixed note cassette - Cartridge that holds the bills, or notes, dispensed by the ATM, which does not come out and needs to be refilled in place. Typically holds 700-1,000 bills. Manufacturers are phasing these out except in the GT3000 TTW machine.

Float - Money within the banking system that is briefly counted twice due to time gaps in registering a deposit or withdrawal.

Freestanding - A style of ATM that has its own foundation and is free of support or attachment.

IAD agreement - A document that defines each party's responsibility for the ordinary course of business in the operation of an ATM machine.

Independent ATM Deployer (IAD) - An individual, group of individuals, a company, or anyone who invests money in an ATM to generate income.

Interbank network - A computer network that enables ATM cards issued by one financial institution to perform ATM transactions through ATMs belonging to another member of the same network.

Interchange - Fee charged by the network your ATM is connected to and imposed by ATM networks on the banks to interconnect their bank with other ATMs.

Interest rates - Proportions of the amounts deposited paid back to the customers.

ISO - Independent Sales Organization; a third-party company that typically sells credit card and/or ATM processing services independently from a bank or financial firm to a business that wants to accept credit card payments.

Journal - A detailed electronic record of all ATM activity. A journal request happens during bank inquiries on reversals.

Just-in-time inventory (JIT) - Management strategy that requires that materials arrive as production is scheduled to begin and no sooner, resulting in the minimum amount of inventory on hand to meet demand.

Kaba Mas, formerly Mas Hamilton lock - A high-security, electronic access control systems lock manufactured by Kaba Mas LLC.

Key - 1. Set of binary numbers used to access and program an ATM. 2. Button on an ATM interface used by the customer to request an action performed by the ATM. 3. A physical key to open the ATM.

LLC - Limited liability company. A business structure that is more formal than a sole proprietorship and offers the owner protection from personal liability a business might incur.

Market gap - Opportunities in the form of voids where a particular service is not currently offered.

Master keys - Sets of binary numbers and letters used to program the ATM, which tethers it to the Terminal ID to register the ATM to the Operator's bank account securely.

Merchant teller - A banker responsible for providing customer service and sales and performing transactions for business customers.

Multi-cassette dispenser - A type of removable cassette which holds two different denominations.

National network - Visa and MasterCard and the Interbank network that works with ATM cards from national banks.

Near-end detection - A unique paper sensor to signal the ATM printer is almost out of paper.

Notes - Banknotes. Bills. Pieces of paper money.

Off-site ATM owner - ATM owner who is not regularly at the location where the ATM is placed.

On-site ATM owner - ATM owner who works in the location where the ATM is placed.

Overhead - Regular business expenses.

Passive income - Income that requires minimal labor and effort to earn and maintain.

Pass-through pricing - Aka buy rate pricing is when an ISO or Sub-ISO passes on all revenue and fees the networks pay. You pay a flat rate for all transaction processing and other services.

Payment Card Industry (PCI) - PCI compliance is an information security standard for handling credit cards from major card brands.

Priority transaction routing - The process of a financial processing system for determining the best route for an electronic financial transaction based on costs and speed.

Profit - The net income collected after investment costs.

Real-time online monitoring - A system that provides updates regarding ATM functions and alerts such as low cash balance.

Refurbished - Used machines that have been cleaned, fixed, retrofitted with the newest software upgrades, and furnished with replacement decals, making it nicer than just a machine categorized as "used" before being sold.

Regional network - Regional Interbank networks that acquire transactions from cards issued by regional bank members.

Reject bin/box/tray - The container within the ATM that holds rejected bills.

Reject box capacity - The maximum number of rejected bills that can be held simultaneously in an ATM.

Removable cassette - Cartridge that holds the bills or notes dispensed by the ATM, which can be taken out of the machine and refilled in another location.

Typically holds 1,000–2,000 bills.

Residuals or Residual Commission - A term that indicates any monthly revenue the ATM operator receives.

Retail Establishment - A store or location that sells goods or services to the general public.

Return on Investment (ROI) - The ratio between net income and investment. A performance measure is used to evaluate the efficiency of an investment. Measure how long it takes to recoup an investment.

Revenue - The gross income collected on an investment.

Revenue share/revenue split - Compensation paid to a store owner in exchange for the space for the ATM.

Reversal - When customers receive no cash or less cash than requested (ATM is low on money or bills were rejected), and they do not receive the right amount of cash, the ATM signals the network to credit their account accordingly.

Route - The locations where you own and/or operate ATMs that you routinely and systematically travel to and from.

Scrip machine - Small countertop machines accepting debit cards but dispensing a voucher for cash. Scrip machines are not supposed to run on ATM networks or have a surcharge fee.

Settlement account - A bank account that receives funds.

Settlement funds - The money used to load the ATM which is deposited to the settlement account by the ATM processor.

Site Location Agreement (SLA) - The agreement, or contract, drawn up between parties that clearly names the business where you are installing the ATM as the location of the machine, your name as the owner, terms, and conditions, and other clauses necessary to maintain the partnership.

Site locator - A person who finds locations interested in having an ATM in or at their location.

Smart transaction routing - A routing policy of some payment processors to efficiently send transactions through the network system.

Sole proprietor/sole proprietorship - Individual entrepreneurship. An enterprise owned and run by one person. The individual and the business are, legally, one and the same.

Spray dispenser - Commonly referred to as the dispenser is a cash dispensing mechanism that dispenses bills one by one into a tray.

Surcharge - The fee you set for each cash withdrawal transaction on your ATM.

Swipe Reader - A data input device that reads data from the magnetic strip on a credit or debit card.

Terminal ID (TID) Number - A Unique number (usually 8-digit) assigned to your ATM, which the ATM processor issues to identify your ATM as it is assigned to your company and used to attribute transactions made through your account to your merchant number.

Through-the-Wall (TTW) - An ATM installed with the back half of the machine (the interface) going into, or through, a wall that protrudes into another room.

Topper/High Topper - A feature that can be added to ATMs to display ads and other graphics.

Transaction - An exchange of service.

Vaulter - A person who loads cash into the ATM.

Vaulting Service - The service provider is responsible for loading money in the ATM and ensuring it doesn't run out.

Vendor relationship - Ongoing interaction with support from the ATM processor---or company---that sells ATMs and other products or services.

Wall mount - A style of ATM that can be conveniently mounted to a wall, table, or counter.

Wireless Device - Also known as a wireless router, it provides 4G data connection from cellular networks. It will use 5G in the future with major carriers such as AT&T, Sprint, Verizon, and T-Mobile.

RESOURCES

I almost didn't call this a resource section. It's more of an "I'm going to save you hours of research and trial and error finding an ATM provider that helps beginners" section, but that was too long for a title.

People often feel a resource section is meant to be an area where the author provides information about who all the various people and players are in the industry and where to find what they need to start the journey.

However, instated of sending you on a research mission, if you really want to jump in and get started, since you read my intro, you learned that I run a business that offers everything I talk about in this book, so I can provide one resource and save you all the trial and errors and mistakes I (and others) have made. You will make mistakes too, and that's good; it's how you succeed. You can't succeed without failures; just don't quit too soon.

I'm Noah. I created my firm, <u>ATMDepot.com</u>, to become a reputable, reliable ATM company that offers ATM sales, service, processing, and ATM Business Training services. We teach ATM Business for beginners with our course, the ATM Business Road Map, because everyone was a beginner once. Professional ball players don't get that way without help, coaching, a good plan, and executing that plan.

We take pride in being an ATM provider that is transparent about the ATM business. We offer how-to videos, scripts, a full-blown training system for ATM Entrepreneurs, and other resources necessary for starting and operating an ATM business.

If you are looking for a complete step-by-step training system, check out How to Start an ATM Business from A - Z, and visit atmbusinessroadmap.com.

ATMBusinessRoadMap.com is an IAD certification course where you will go through 9 Modules in 60 Video Lessons that go over everything you need to know to start your ATM Business from nothing to making money. Visit the website for more information. Since this book is also included in the course but you already purchased it, I'm offering anyone that bought the book a very special discount should you decide to purchases the course. Simply leave a book review on Amazon and send your review link to atmbusinessroadmap@gmail.com to receive a special coupon code for the course.

If you are reading a hard copy of this book offline, and want to jump right in and access the resources, simply use your phone to scan this QR code.

You can browse equipment options and get the ATM machine you want by completing an equipment order form.

Here are some of the top brand new ATM machine recommendations:

- Hyosung Halo II - https://atm.noahwieder.com/2600se
- Hyosung Force - https://atm.noahwieder.com/2800se
- Genmega G2500 - https://atm.noahwieder.com/g2500
- Genmega Nova - https://atm.noahwieder.com/nova

ATM providers that offer real-time online usage access:

You can contact these ATM providers if you prefer to deal with a large corporation if you don't think ATMDepot.com is right for you.

1. Columbus Data - https://columbusdata.net/

2. Cardtronics (now NCR but mobile contact) https://resources.atmdepot.com/ncrATM (Access from Cell Phone for - USA & Canada)

3. NCR - https://www.ncr.com/atm-network

4. FISERV - https://resources.atmdepot.com/fiserv

Camera system options: Many retailers offer cameras. Here are some of the ones I've used with success that have a smartphone app so you can check in:

Any Ring Camera from Amazon

Indoor Camera Suggestions - https://resources.atmdepot.com/indoorcamera

Outdoor Camera Suggestions - https://resources.atmdepot.com/outdoorcamera

Interchange: Depending on your transaction volume and the level of help you need, my firm ATMDepot.com does offer the option to receive interchange or a flat per transaction buy rate with enough transaction volume.

Buy rate for transaction processing:

Once you have been in the ATM business a while and require less and less support, there are opportunities to obtain flat rate pricing if you are doing enough transactions. Everyone upstream has a flat rate. Your rate, like anything else in the world, is based on your consumption. Imagine how cheap you'd get hot dogs if you ate as many hot dogs as Costco sells yearly. It's the same principle. Everyone helping you has expenses, and there is only so much interchange to go around—and that's also getting reduced every year. So, getting 100% of the surcharge without any fees is a pretty safe bet. Once you start generating five, ten or even fifteen thousand surcharge transactions monthly, you can evaluate whether switching to a flat buy rate would help you or cost you. Evaluate everything. If you get a flat buy rate, you'll probably have to pay small onboarding fees, or a statement fee, or perhaps pass-through network fees, and other possible charges. We see statements from many companies with hidden fees all the time. Don't go all in, either. If you negotiate a flat rate, add a new machine and evaluate. Don't move all your machines over to new rates without evaluation. Take it from someone who's been doing this for 30 years.

Wireless Devices:

There are several options for ATM wireless. I prefer In-Hand routers.

You can undoubtedly do a Google search to find what you're looking for. I suggest getting wireless devices and services from the same ATM vendor so that no one points fingers. Even if it's a few bucks difference, the headache of having different vendors isn't worth a couple of bucks a month when troubleshooting issues between one vendor or multiple vendors. We offer competitive rates and outstanding training and support if you use my firm, ATMDepot.com as your ATM vendor.

Multi-carrier SIM models:

This is only necessary if you have intermittent service from one particular carrier, you move the ATM between events, or you have a mobile ATM (in a trailer or kiosk you move). Ask your ATM provider if they offer these if you need them. Otherwise, contact ATMDepot.com if you need help.

Surrounds, Wraps, and Decals:

TPI Texas.com https://tpitexas.com/ offers wooden surrounds and security enclosures.

DASH ATM https://www.dashatm.com/ security enclosures and canopies are used by many financial institutions.

GetBranded.com https://getbranded.com/ offers ATM wraps, topper inserts, banners, signs, and more.

ATMDepot.com offers standard and custom decal sheets and ATM model-specific decals.

Third Party Media Companies:

JBC Media Box - https://jbcmediabox.com/atm/

Smartcast Media - https://smartcastmedia.com/

Installation Equipment:

½" x 4 ¼" Wedge Anchors - https://resources.atmdepot.com/Wedge-Anchors

⅜" x 3 ¾" Stainless Steel Wedge - https://resources.atmdepot.com/Stainless-Steel-Wedge

Surge Protector over 650VA - https://resources.atmdepot.com/SurgeProtector

Wedge and Installation Tips - https://resources.atmdepot.com/wedgeinstallationtips

ATM Insurance:

<u>Marshall & Sterling</u> developed an insurance program to protect you against losing your ATM and the money inside. They offer coverage, including basic insurance areas, crime, property, and liability. Coverage depends on the total number of machines, the maximum amount of cash per machine, and the replacement cost of each machine.

Want to know more about other ways to operate your ATM business? Check out the ATMDepot.com Members Area.

ATMDepot.com Members Area

Most of the following information is available on ATMDepot.com, its blog, one of its YouTube Channels (<u>ATM Processing</u> or <u>ATM Depot</u>), or Facebook page (<u>ATM Depot HQ</u>).

If you received this book as part of your atmbusinessroadmap.com membership you receive 12 months free access to the ATMDepot.com member area. Please <u>contact us</u> if you need help.

ATM Processing Channel on YouTube:
https://resources.atmdepot.com/ATM-Processing-Channel

If you plan to work with ATMDepot.com, everyone there will welcome the chance to help you succeed.

How To Load Cash Video: Videos are available that will walk you through how to load cash, the settlement process, and other important functions: https://resources.atmdepot.com/HowToLoadCash

Cash Management and Cash Balancing: This document will guide you on how to load cash on your ATM: https://resources.atmdepot.com/HowToLoadCash

How Your ATM Gets Delivered: This video shows how the ATM arrives, what to look for when it arrives, and what to check to ensure it has arrived in working order.

How To Resolve Common ATM Related Issues: This video explains ATM error codes for common issues with typical resolutions.

The exclusive <u>Members Area</u> is available to Independent ATM Deployers wanting access to specific information. This is an example of what our IADs can find in our Members Area.

Besides our 24/7 technical support, our IAD Basic and ATM Business Road Map course include:

How-to and help videos on topics such as:

- What to Say to Store Owners
- How and Where to Find Good ATM Locations
- How to Change the ATM Lock Combo
- What are Master Keys and Convelops
- How to Conduct Programming
- And much more

How-to and helpful audio files for listening on the go:

- Step by Step Instructions on how to program a Hyosung Halo
- Sales Scripts
- Overcoming Objections
- And much more

Document Samples and Templates (scan QR Code for access):

- Equipment Order Forms
- Merchant Applications
- ACH forms
- Placement Agreement Samples
- Site Location Agreement (SLA)

Scan the QR Code to download fillable pdf copies.

BONUS RESOURCES
Sample Sales Script:

These scripts help you to understand how to approach a building or retail owners. It will also help you know what to say, how to handle objections, etc.

We update the <u>Members Area</u> (atmdepot.com/members) information to stay current. When new information is added, or old and outdated information is purged, the Members Area stays up-to-date, so you only get the information that matters. No hype, no fluff.

Note that lifetime members of the atmbusinessroadmap.com receive 12 months free access to the member area listed above.

Here is one of the sample scripts:

How to Get a Store Owner's Contact Info

Don't make this complicated; match the owner's energy once you know who they are. If there is more than one owner, business partner, or a couple that owns it together, whoever they are, identify the decision maker (usually the one with the objections...haha) and try to match their energy. If you're excited and like to talk fast (how I get sometimes), tell yourself to calm down if the person you're speaking to doesn't have the same energy or excitement.

It also depends on the time of day and the type of store. A nightclub owner will have a different mood than a barbershop owner. Sometimes the owners have people to make these decisions if it's a retailer with multiple establishments. You need to get to those people.

Practice the pitch you're comfortable with and test different ones until you get the owner's contact info.

This works great for local retailers that you've been a customer of. If you're not a customer and want to use this introduction, become a customer first; otherwise, try the optional "not a customer yet elevator script":

Hello, my name is [Your Name]. I've been to your place several times and am a big fan.

If you haven't been there, but your friend, spouse, or whoever has, then say that:

Hello, my name is [Noah], and my wife absolutely loves your [name of product or service she used]. We are both big fans. (If it's a restaurant/bar, find their signature cocktail or most popular appetizer or dish and try it.)

When you try their most popular appetizer, pizza, or happy hour, or if you visit a barbershop, tattoo place, or nail salon, if they have a best-selling product, then you can sincerely talk about it. Whatever it is, you get the idea.

Link something they offer (whatever you bought) to your introduction. They will subconsciously agree with your statement since you compliment their service or product.

Now you have their attention. So then you say....

I'm in the ATM business and wanted to ask who is the best person to speak with about providing you with a free ATM machine? Your customers will have access to cash to pay for tips, and it helps reduce your high credit card fees. It's completely free.

You can also say: I happen to be in the ATM business. I wanted to talk to an owner about possibly setting up a free ATM to give your customers access to cash. (I find that merchants like to qualify for free stuff, so test which of these scripts works better for you or come up with something more natural. Both of these are proven to work.)

Then pause and wait for an objection, see if they offer the owner's name and some way to reach them or confess and tell you they are the owner.

If you pause and they don't respond (count to 5; it will seem like forever, but give them a chance to process what you said), continue with...

...We also share the surcharge commission with the location, so the ATM helps the owner and employees. Could you tell me the best way to contact the owner?

Pause again...

Occasionally, you might even be talking to the owner and not know it. They will either engage with you, ask more questions about how your program works, give you the contact info, or come up with an objection. Maybe the owner told them never to give out their info.

They might say, "Why don't you leave me your card, and I'll give it to the owner?" At that point, if you keep talking, you're wasting your time. This might be the best time to ask for the owner's name or the best person to connect with the next time you pass by.

Be sure you have business cards or just a simple brochure of your ATM Placement Program with your contact info on it. Don't spend much on fancy brochures when you first start if you plan to walk in cold (without an appointment or letting anyone know you're coming). You might need to hit 20 or 30 locations or more to get a half dozen leads.

If you can't get the contact info and they want you to leave your contact info, you don't need a fancy brochure. A simple sheet of paper with your program and contact info is all you need to start. If you can't get the owner's name, get the name of the person you spoke with and their position.

Then in a few days, go back and buy something if the person you spoke with is working. Say hi to them and strike up a conversation. Ask them again for the owner's contact info if you haven't heard from them. Switch up your script and use the "qualify for a free ATM" line.

Sometimes it takes a few trips to develop rapport and trust. Suppose you think it will be a good location. In that case, you can use some online tools to find the owner's contact info. Don't give up until they tell you they aren't interested.

Practice your pitch, and get it down so it rolls off your tongue naturally.

Another way to get the owner's info is a quick elevator pitch:

In the store - elevator script:

Hi, I'm the owner of [your company name]. We are a local business that offers a limited number of retailers in the area a free ATM if they qualify. Who is the best person to speak with to see if you qualify for a free ATM?

If they tell you who the person is but don't offer a way to contact them, then say, Okay, how can I contact them directly to see if you qualify? (Pause. Do they offer the contact info? If they say anything other than the contact info, proceed.)

When is it a good time to reach them? (Pause. Did they tell you? If not, proceed.)

Will they be there tomorrow, or is there a better day and time to meet them?

Telemarketing version:

Hi, I'm the owner of [your company name]. I own a local business that offers qualified retailers in the area a free ATM. Would you be the person to speak with about that?

(Yes) Great. I'd love to meet you for a few minutes to see if you qualify. Would tomorrow or [suggest another day] at [select a morning and afternoon time] work? Or ask: What's a good day and time to come by to meet you?

Telemarketing Objections: I already have an ATM.

Response: Oh, that's fantastic. How long have you owned and operated it?

[NOTE:] If they answer, that's a signal that they may be willing to talk, and you should use that opportunity to see if there is some way to do business. If they don't own or operate it and you can find out that someone else does, ask qualifying questions like:

Oh, nice; how long have they been doing that for ya?

(If they say years)

Ah, I like to hear about loyal customers. That's great.

(Keep the conversation going)

Are they still happy with it?

Are they having any issues?

Do they have a newer model ATM?

(At some point, mention that you provide service and cash vaulting.)

Perhaps, they'd rather have an ATM service handle some things. Have they updated the ATM recently, firmware, or software? Do they know how to load graphics to take full advantage of the marketing? (Maybe offer some local marketing while you're already looking for ATM places; you can use their ATM as an opportunity to cross-sell or promote coupons.)

[NOTE:] If they run it themselves, ask yourself if they are tired of doing that. You can take over cash loading to get in the door if they are tired of that job. Ensure they have an alarm and ask about cameras, and check the ATM security before you decide to take over cash loading only. Ask if they've ever had a break-in.

Getting them to Qualify:

The idea of a cold call or walk-in is to get them to settle on an agreed-upon time to have an in-person discussion about how they qualify for a free ATM placement.

If they ask you, "How do I qualify," at any point, that is an invitation. When telemarketing, using your adopted version of the above. If/when they ask you how they can qualify over the phone, that is your open invitation. What you say next matters most so you can meet them in their store at a mutually convenient time.

Be sure you have time to go there before your first meeting if you've never been there. Check out the store on Google Maps or another map app to zoom in and look around the neighborhood. Look up statistics on the traffic at intersections to familiarize yourself with the area.

If you are in person already, you can say, "I can sit down with you now if that is convenient. Do you have an office or table we can use?" Most people will try to brush you off or make excuses. People are busy, skeptical, and want to be sold. If you don't enjoy selling, even though you aren't selling anything, you must learn that you're selling yourself. When you do sit down with the proprietor, don't sit opposite them or across the table. Try to sit next to them or caddy-corner so you can show them your presentation or talk with them more casually at that point. You don't want the table to be a barrier between you and whoever you're negotiating (collaborating) with.

Now your true friendly professionalism comes into play. I like to be official and have a form in a folder or use the SurveyMonkey app to look professional. You can set up a free account or go old school, make a form, and keep track manually. Both have advantages, but just use what you're comfortable with as long as you use some method and don't just wing it. You're getting the knowledge; then you'll make a plan. You'll consistently execute the plan to perfect it. Ask...

Q: Approximately how many customers do you serve daily (if it's not a service business, or they aren't sure what you're asking, then say):

Q: How many people come in on average, or how many tickets do you ring up? Q: What about weekends?

Q: How many tickets do you get on your busiest day?

You want the average to be at least 50 for a nail salon or barbershop. That's about 1,500 people per month, and if many are regulars, that should get you 4-5 uses daily.

A tattoo shop usually doesn't get as many customers unless they have a gamer area where people might wait or take a break from the needlework. But if they have at least 30 customers daily, and 3 use the ATM, it's still a decent ROI.

Bars, restaurants, nightclubs, and similar service businesses will serve many more customers daily—usually 100+ for smaller ones. A fast or quick-service restaurant might serve 250-400 meals daily or more.

Weed dispensaries will typically have high traffic (pun intended). But most can't accept credit cards yet, and if they take debit as an ATM, they are doing it illegally.

Parking lots, off-site car rentals, manufacturing facilities with many employees, or any location that services hundreds of people daily should be a decent spot with the proper signage, incentives (like a coupon), and a clean machine with a big display.

Once you have enough information and see how many people come in while you are there, do your own due diligence. Does it seem like a busy enough place? If it's a nail salon, do they have many chairs, or are they all occupied? What is the busiest day? Go visit during the busiest time. Do customers ask about the closest ATM? Now it's time to decide if the location has qualified, whether you are satisfied with the answers and want to proceed.

For Further Reading

2001 Article by Noah Wieder Featured in *Transaction World*: "Are ATMs the New Plastic?" - https://www.academia.edu/41887587/Transaction_World_Article_on_ATM_Machines_-_Author_Noah_Wieder

"The Best Banks for ATM Business" - https://atmdepot.com/best-banks-for-atm-business/

Highest ATM Fees in Various Cities - https://www.bankrate.com/banking/cities-with-highest-atm-fees/

www.ingramcontent.com/pod-product-compliance
Lightning Source LLC
Chambersburg PA
CBHW071154290526
45796CB00007B/42